The Cathedral Builder

A Biography of J. Irwin Miller

Charles E. Mitchell Rentschler

authorHOUSE®

AuthorHouse™
1663 Liberty Drive
Bloomington, IN 47403
www.authorhouse.com
Phone: 1-800-839-8640

This book is a work of non-fiction. Unless otherwise noted, the author and the publisher
make no explicit guarantees as to the accuracy of the information contained in this book
and in some cases, names of people and places have been altered to protect their privacy.

Published by AuthorHouse 12/17/2014

ISBN: 978-1-4969-5610-1 (sc)
ISBN: 978-1-4969-5611-8 (hc)
ISBN: 978-1-4969-5609-5 (e)

Library of Congress Control Number: 2014921291

Any people depicted in stock imagery provided by Thinkstock are models,
and such images are being used for illustrative purposes only.
Certain stock imagery © Thinkstock.

This book is printed on acid-free paper.

*To my wife, Suzie, our three children, their
spouses, and our three grandchildren*

Contents

Photographed in his 40s, Miller exuded naval
bearing from his wartime experience.
Provided by the Indiana Historical Society

Prologue

J. Irwin Miller was a bit of a paradox. He was fiercely competitive both in business and leisure, yet he was loath to fire or demote people who weren't performing.[1] He was fluent in the dead languages—Latin and Greek—but never bothered learning French, German, or Spanish.[2] He was a lifelong Republican, nominally, but inclined toward socialism. He rarely told people what to do, preferring to ask them questions until they figured things out for themselves.[3] He was a self-proclaimed "big-picture guy," yet he could dive deeply into such details as the shrubbery outside a new Cummins facility in Minnesota[4] or the stationery for North Christian Church.[5]

Yet J. Irwin Miller was a consummate manager of his time. He was able to leverage himself by keeping his office remote from his business and pro bono interests, delegating work to highly intelligent, hardworking aides, minimizing staff meetings, and avoiding customer visits, among other things.[6]

The thoughtful arrangement of his time permitted Miller to do what his religion, Christian Church (Disciples of Christ), instructed its members to do—preach the word of God (which he did in 164 speeches he wrote and delivered over his lifetime) and perform "good works," mainly, in addition to serving as CEO of Cummins Engine twenty-six years, helping guide the National Council of Churches, Yale University, and the Ford Foundation. Yet there was still time to raise his family, take summer and winter vacations, travel to faraway places, and entertain interesting people.

But people who knew Miller well defined him, above all else, as a Christian. His successor as Cummins's CEO, Henry B. Schacht, described his longtime boss as a "deeply religious human being [whose] most simple philosophy is to do unto others as you would have others be responsible to you. He is a deeply philosophical person and well schooled in Christian beliefs, and he practices them every day."[7]

Drawing from a deep wellspring of Christianity on both sides of his family (his two grandfathers were ministers), Miller was always concerned about the "other guy"—championing the rights and needs of people of color, women, and gays decades before it was expected and accepted, doing what he could for the poor, looking out for the "hourlies" instead of their supervisors in his factories, the enlisted instead of the officers in the navy, and the downtrodden instead of the well-off in the world in general. Each year, Miller gave 35 percent of his income and 5 percent of Cummins's profits to charity.

Ed Booth, his assistant for several years in the 1970s, says the most impressive thing about his boss was "his deep sense of moral outrage at injustice done to others."[8] Susan Hanafee, author of *Red, Black and Global*, recounting the 2001 closure of Cummins's original plant in Columbus, Indiana, recalls Miller's reaction: "Just make sure you treat the people right."[9] Carolyn McKin Spicer, who was the housekeeper and cook for the Millers for twenty years toward the end of their lives, said, "I've never known anyone as kind, as compassionate, and as caring [as Miller]."[10]

An example of Miller's selflessness is the story of his interment as personally told to us by John Bean, his since-deceased, longtime pastor. He recalled that "Miller wanted to be buried on the grounds of North Christian Church" (of which Miller was far and away the biggest benefactor). "He wanted the congregation to let him construct a crypt either underneath the church or in the woods, but the congregation wouldn't go for it." So Miller gently backed off.[11] He would be laid to rest in his family plot in Columbus's City Cemetery under a modest headstone not fifteen yards from Sixteenth Street.

Miller, as a Christian, believed payback for leading an exemplary life on earth was spending eternity in heaven. Six days before his eighty-fifth birthday, addressing a group of architects in Indianapolis, he exhorted them "to emulate the cathedral builders of the twelfth century... laying in their lifetime no more than footings and foundations, if this is all they could get done," believing they could look down on their completed church from heaven when they left this life.[12]

Just five years earlier, in the riskiest financial act of his lifetime, Miller had pledged nearly 60 percent of his family's net worth to rescue Cummins from a hostile takeover and likely liquidation. "[Cummins's] long-term future," he continued, "will probably not be fully realized in my lifetime, but I am excited about its possibility and the jobs it will create, whether I am around or not."[13]

1

A Long Line of Christians and Capitalists

In 1909, the year J. Irwin Miller was born, the most imposing building in his hometown of Columbus, Indiana, was its 150-foot-tall Italianate courthouse.[1] It took up a full city block and would likely be the first object to catch the eye of anyone visiting the seat of Bartholomew County.

However, huge courthouses were common in the state. By 1900, sixty of Indiana's ninety-two counties had erected new government buildings in a frenzied drive to be the biggest, gaudiest, or most costly.[2] Columbus's downtown at the time consisted of just three or four square blocks with a couple dozen stores to serve the surrounding area—predominantly farming, with some light manufacturing.

The soil in Bartholomew County was not nearly as black and fertile as the soil in the northwest part of Indiana, but it still appealed to the Scotch-Irish who'd moved up from Kentucky for its cheap land—the incentive was very good to clear forty to fifty acres.[3]

The Midwest was on the verge of a boom as Americans put themselves in cars en masse with the arrival of the assembly line for Henry Ford's Model T. But "the citizens of Bartholomew County witnessed industrialization mainly from a distance—the population of Columbus increased by a mere 860 persons in the first two decades in the new century... to fewer than 9,000 residents, making it the 36th largest community in the state,"[4] a mere backwater.

The town did have passenger rail service—not only the steam-powered Pennsylvania but also an electric interurban (the Columbus, Indianapolis & Southern Traction Co.) that, interestingly, paralleled each other forty miles north to Indianapolis and twenty-five mile south to Seymour. Thus, few that there were (usually wealthy) travelers going east (say, New York City) or west (say, Saint Louis) would need to connect either through Indianapolis or Seymour.[5]

As a rule, people in Columbus and in the country got around locally either on foot or horse and buggy—cars were far too expensive and unreliable and stored inside in winter since roads were often impassable. In fact, decades later, Miller recalled that "there was a hitching rack around the west side of the courthouse when I was a little boy, and I remember teams of oxen hitched there because [it] was the only way to get to town from Brown County [to the west] during the winter months."[6]

Columbus' Italianate courthouse was tallest building
in town in 1909, the year Miller was born.
Provided by Rhonda Bolner, Columbus, Indiana

An exception was Columbus's most prominent citizen and leading banker, and Irwin Miller's great-grandfather Joseph Ireland Irwin. A year before young Irwin was born, he had purchased a large eight-cylinder Packard car.

At eighty, Joseph Ireland Irwin was retired and widowed, and his success was hard won. He had grown up on a hardscrabble farm north of Columbus, but using profits from a succession of real-estate deals, he had managed to buy a dry goods store, wherein he created a bank (ultimately Irwin Bank). He later teamed up with his only son, William Glanton Irwin (W. G.), in building the Interurban that was such a success "that he attracted a buyer for his line, none other than Sam Insull, who paid well for the CI&S in 1912, at just about the time that W. G. was cannily deciding that the automobile was turning Interurban railroads into a poor business."[7] W. G. turned his attention to Irwin Bank, located kitty-corner across from the courthouse at Third and Washington Streets.

The family came from staunchly egalitarian roots, and in Bartholomew County during the Civil War, this raised a red flag. Bartholomew was Southern in sympathy and never gave Lincoln a plurality of votes in either 1860 or 1864, when he ran for president. Joseph Irwin, however, was known as so strong an opponent of slavery and so determined a proponent of the Union that the local cell of Copperheads marked him for assassination. The attempt was made, but it failed. Much later, Irwin's mother, Nettie, once asked her grandfather on his deathbed if he was afraid to die. His response was this: "Why? No one could have come into this world more helpless than I, nor had a happier life. I'm sure I'll make out as well in whatever comes next."[8] Joseph Ireland Irwin even named his first son, Charles Sumner Irwin, after the abolitionist senator from Massachusetts.

Meanwhile, on the Sweeney side, his maternal great-grandfather Guyrn Sweeney, an innkeeper from Kentucky, "decided he didn't want to raise his already large family in a slave state, and so moved them all to Illinois, with no assurance that he could make a living there."

The lead story in Columbus's newspaper, the *Evening Republican*, April 19, 1909—five weeks before Miller's birth—reveals much about Guyrn's son, Zachary Taylor Sweeney, a retired minister of Christian Church (Disciples of Christ). The paper had published a story about a Jewish immigrant from Romania who had come to the United States to start a new life. After earning some money, the immigrant sent for his wife and children—but his youngest son was refused entry into the country because of head lice. When the Ellis Island hospital began to charge the man for his son's expenses, he simply couldn't keep up, and the boy was sent back to Romania.

The next day, the *Evening Republican* reported the following:

> This story so enraged Mr. Sweeney that he sent the following letter to President [Taft]:

> *I am exceedingly anxious to know if anyone in the service of the United States government could be a party to such a transaction. If that little child has been deported because there was no means to pay the hospital expenses, I should like to have you cable for the child's return and have it placed in the hospital, and I will be personally responsible for its expenses until some humane disposition has been made of it. Senator Hemingway or Senator Beveridge[9] can advise you whether I am responsible for my promises... Z. T. Sweeney.[10]*

Five days later, when Sweeney is told "the government has not funds for such expense,"[11] he responds. "If there is no means available for the care of a child under such circumstances, there ought to be," he writes. "I shall make it my business to bombard Congress until money is placed at the discretion of the Secretary to care for children in such circumstances."[12]

Three blocks east and two blocks north of the courthouse at 608 Fifth Street was the Irwin household. It was one of the town's nicest homes, built by Joseph himself in 1864.

The home was in fact a veritable family castle, as, at one point, in addition to Joseph Ireland and W. G. Irwin, six other family members shared the residence: W. G.'s sister, Linnie, and her husband, Z. T. Sweeney, their single daughter, Elsie; their married daughter, Nettie, and her husband, Hugh T. Miller, an active politician (and son of another Disciples minister) and their three-year-old daughter, Clementine.

The mansion, remodeled in 1890, was probably confining for the extended family as well as three or four young black and/or Irish immigrant servants (as they were called) to cook and clean. However, in 1910/11, the third floor was expanded, elevator added, and large Italianate garden created.

One day in 1908, Joseph Ireland decided that he wanted to hire a mechanic-chauffeur to maintain the Packard and drive him places. His daughter Linnie had learned that the son of one of her Sunday school students, Clessie Cummins, might be suitable for the job. She arranged for her brother, W. G., to take Clessie for a test drive one evening. We join the story recounted in *The Engine That Could*, a company-sponsored history published in 1997:

> There was one problem: Clessie's size, relative to the car [stored on blocks in a barn near the Irwin mansion]. Clessie, small in stature, managed to lower the huge automobile to the ground, but then faced a much more difficult challenge. The electric self-starter was not commercially available in the United States until 1912. It was reasonable to wonder—as both W. G. and Clessie did that day—whether a slight, 110-pound teenager could hand-crank the heavy Packard engine. After several tries, the answer was obvious. He could not.

Starting the car surely was a job requirement. In desperation, Clessie resorted to a trick he knew from boating. He dipped a rag into the gas tank, squeezed a few drops of fuel into each cylinder priming cup, rocked the engine again, and fired the ignition spark. It worked.[13]

Clessie glanced at W. G. "He was beaming," Clessie remembers. "'I'd rather have a man anytime who could use his head in place of his back,' he shouted about the engine's roar."[14] Much later, when Clessie knew more about engine mechanics, he noted the 'astronomical odds against such a procedure being successful with a big engine.' It was luck as much as ingenuity that won him his first job with the Irwins.[15]

For a few years, Clessie worked for the Irwins as a part-time mechanic and driver, but W. G. eventually set him up in a machine shop where Clessie Cummins pursued his interest of developing diesel-engine technology. It was here that the Cummins Engine Company was founded in 1919.

Linnie's daughter, Nettie, and her husband, Hugh T. Miller, had moved into the mansion with their young daughter, Clementine. Hugh's promising-looking political career as a state representative (from 1902 to 1903) and then lieutenant governor (from 1904 to 1909) involved near-constant travel that left his bride and child alone much of the time. J. Irwin Miller was born in the mansion on May 26, 1909.

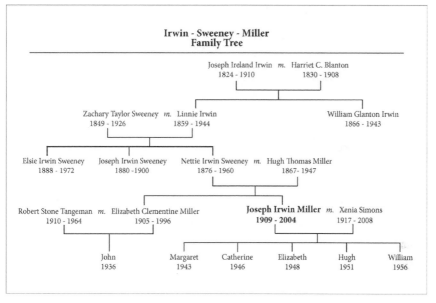

Irwin - Sweeney - Miller Family Tree

Joseph Ireland Irwin *m.* Harriet C. Blanton
1824 - 1910 · 1830 - 1908

Zachary Taylor Sweeney *m.* Linnie Irwin
1849 - 1926 · 1859 - 1944

William Glanton Irwin
1866 - 1943

Elsie Irwin Sweeney
1888 - 1972

Joseph Irwin Sweeney
1880 -1900

Nettie Irwin Sweeney *m.* Hugh Thomas Miller
1876 - 1960 · 1867- 1947

Robert Stone Tangeman *m.* Elizabeth Clementine Miller
1910 - 1964 · 1905 - 1996

Joseph Irwin Miller *m.* Xenia Simons
1909 - 2004 · 1917 - 2008

John
1936

Margaret
1943

Catherine
1946

Elizabeth
1948

Hugh
1951

William
1956

Scotch-Irish ancestry provided Miller a life-long religious compass.
Provided by the Indiana Historical Society

Four years younger than his sister, Clementine, young Miller naturally would get a great deal of love and attention. He was the sole male heir and not just for his generation but also for the one ahead, as his uncle, Joseph II, Linnie's only son, had died nine years before Miller's birth in a tragic swimming accident at age twenty.[16]

So great was their elation over a new male heir that the family named young Miller "Joseph" after the patriarch. But the family quickly realized that they could not bear to call him "Joe," because it brought back too many memories and involved too much pain. So they would use his middle name, Irwin, shortening the first name to the initial *J*.[17]

If not for his father's subsequent health problems, young Miller might have grown up in Washington, DC. Hugh was narrowly defeated as the Republican candidate for US Senate from Indiana in 1914 and seen as a shoo-in for the other US Senate seat in 1916, and he contracted tuberculosis. Rather than serve a term or longer in Washington (where young Miller might have spent his years through adolescence), his father worked in Columbus at the family bank as his health permitted.[18]

Miller was profoundly influenced by his family and ancestry. Obviously, the forebears who had most impact on Miller were those six with whom he grew up at 608 Fifth Street. Miller's sister, Clementine, recalled that from the time her brother could sit in a chair until he went off to boarding school, aged fourteen, "we always ate three family meals together—breakfast, dinner, and supper, and we [her brother and she] sat there and listened... we began to take on adult manners in ways of dealing with people." That sometimes included visitors from overseas.[19]

Dinner-table conversation ran the gamut—politics, business, religion, and philosophy, as well as day-to-day occurrences. And each Sunday dinner, Miller recalled in that interview, "the sermon was analyzed and reanalyzed." No one left the table to clean the dishes, get the next course, or help oneself to seconds—there were servants to do those chores. And alcohol was not permitted in the Irwin home.[20] "The females were equally strong, equally influential, whether in church, community, or business," he said. "No move would be made unless there was family consensus."

"In 1910–1915, the men in the household were active proponents of women's suffrage, and the women of the family were only mildly interested—much more active in feeding and clothing the poor and finding jobs for young men."[21] "The family was always strongly supportive of Jews, and I can remember that an anti-Semitic statement or hint was a genuine no-no at the dinner table."[22]

Perhaps less formal but sometimes more intense were the family's vacations each summer at Lake Rousseau in the Muskoka region of northern Ontario, which started with the purchase of a house there by Joseph I. Irwin in 1909, the year of Miller's birth.

Later in his life, Miller wrote in longhand his recollections of his childhood growing up at 608 Fifth Street in an uncharacteristically breezy (perhaps somewhat tongue in cheek) account:

[Great-uncle] W. G. was a very gregarious and personally charming bachelor who failed to get married out of laziness. But he was, in this unusual household, surrounded with all the appearances of marriage— two small children; women to keep house and provide excellent meals.

His sister, Linnie, my [maternal] grandmother, was married impulsively at 16 [to Z. T. Sweeney] instead of going to Vassar as her father wished. She was extraordinarily close to her brother and actively disapproved of any woman in whom he showed an interest...

Miller says he brought all his teenage questions to his maternal grandfather, Z. T. Sweeney, as no question seemed to shock him. By 1909, retired as minister of Columbus's Tabernacle Christian Church (predecessor to First Christian), Sweeney had served several years as general consul to Istanbul and, an avid conservationist, was head of Indiana's Fish and Game Department.

"His relations with his wife, my grandmother [Linnie], I never quite understood. She was always closer to her family [extended] than to her husband, who she always addressed as 'Mr. Sweeney.' She once told me that the reason she got married at age sixteen was to be able to go to 'the Greeks' [Zaharako's] and buy ice cream whenever she wanted without having to ask her mother."

Early on, women had a profound impact on Miller's upbringing. He wrote that after the tragic death of his uncle Joe, his grandmother Linnie "spent the rest of her life working with and for young men in the community who needed jobs or any kind of help. Sometimes she failed or was taken to the cleaners, but in my memory, she allowed nothing to divert her."

As he got older, Miller began to look to his elders in shaping his own world views. "On fishing trips with Grandfather Sweeney, I used to question him endlessly and critically. He was a learned man. His answers were impressive, but [he would say] 'Son, don't accept this simply because I say it. Finally you will have to think out each of these matters for yourself.'"[23]

But it was his own father, Hugh, who instilled Miller with true faith. Miller later declared, "Each of us has known Christlike persons. My own father was one. You simply could not give voice to a shabby, self-centered thought in his presence. Even his silence shamed and enlightened you."[24] "[He] was often an uncomfortable man with whom to talk."[25]

"My father set scholastic records at Butler [then did graduate studies at Middlebury and the Sorbonne]... and loved learning all his life. If a word or concept came up at the dinner table [that he did not understand], he would often get up to go to the encyclopedia before returning to his meal. At this point in my life [aged sixteen], I honestly thought he knew everything there was to know... he never paraded his knowledge, though... I received only one clue as to how my mother [Nettie] felt about this... I heard a [female] friend exclaim to my mother that 'Mr. Miller is surely the smartest man I know.' To this, my mother's reply was 'Yes, and he is not entirely unaware of the fact.'"

Miller's own son Will would later say about his father: "Dad had a real sense of coming from tradition. The family background, though, did not confer on him either a right or a privilege, but a responsibility."[26]

Summarizing the effect of growing up at 608 Fifth Street, Miller recalled, "I entered business because I had been born and raised in a household in which business matters were openly and constantly discussed. I was also raised in a household in which the practical application of Christianity was openly and constantly discussed. I suppose the combination of these has a great deal of influence on a person."[27]

"I must confess," Miller wrote ten years later, "in my earlier decades, the choice was inherited, relatively unexamined, and hence watery at best. As the years have passed, the inheritance has been converted from the accepted and unexamined to a slowly changed but individually tested commitment and guide."[28]

But business was in this family's blood. Great-grandfather Joseph I. Irwin and Great-uncle W. G. Irwin were essentially entrepreneurs, with great-grandfather Joseph establishing the bank and W. G. forming the Interurban and helping start Union Starch, Purity Stores, and Cummins Engine. Miller, by contrast, was a manager.

And in 1919, when Miller was ten years old, Cummins Engine Company was organized, half owned by Clessie and half by W. G. and Linnie. It was through her insistence that the family invested and kept investing, in good times or bad, in Clessie Cummins. Her word was "Don't explain, fix the problem, do something." Neither she nor her brother received or expected to receive during their lifetime any return on that considerable investment. Her life to the day of her death was to create good jobs for young men in our community… and to follow up and have a care for each young man who came to her notice.[29]

Clessie's goal for the engine company, as he would later remind his investors in 1939 (20 years after its inception), was to first "create a school… setting down as No. 1 matter of policy the building of as nearly a perfect machine as is humanly possible… second, training and developing of the manpower of the community… and third… a non-paternal, but very earnest interest… in the affairs of the employees."[30]

Confirming Clessie's understanding, three days later came W. G.'s handwritten response: "All of us are greatly pleased with your reply to the policy statement… had it not been our desire to have a place to develop the young men around Columbus we should not have taken the risks that we did."[31]

Thus, laid bare, Cummins Engine was organized as a "charity" to help the local community. Accordingly, it needn't necessarily produce a profit, *and it did not* for its first seventeen years (when its main benefactors, W. G. and Linnie, were respectively, seventy-one and seventy-eight years old). Has there ever been in the annals of American business history a better example of patient capitalism?

As Miller recalled, "Clessie first asked W. G. for $10,000, then kept asking for $10,000 more, but after $2 million [was advanced], it still didn't work."[32] It was in fact losing money.

So what was going on? Obviously, W. G. was wealthy. The (wholly-owned) Irwin Bank and the Union Starch & Refining Company (78 percent owned) were his very profitable businesses, and there was steady income from leasing the Interurban assets to Sam Insull, plus real-estate deals in the area.

Next, as an entrepreneur, he came to expect and learn to deal with occasional losses. For example, his two companies making mercury electric switches went broke. His great-nephew, Miller, said "Unc" claimed "if you hit one in five, you were doing well."[33]

Very importantly, W. G. and Clessie had a "very, very close relationship."[34] Miller quoted W. G. as saying, "Some people get their kicks backing Broadway shows. I get my kicks out of backing Clessie Cummins."[35] Clessie routinely was "doing a sales job" on W. G., frequently lunching at 608 Fifth Street. When W. G. was told (in the midthirties) that the engine company for the first time had shipped over $1 million in a month, he could only say, over and over, "My, my, my…," according to Ray Boll, longtime head of sales.[36]

In a file memo written years later, Miller wrote, "These two were very close and genuinely fond of each other. Clessie was proud of W. G.'s standing and of the position this gave him… W. G., in turn, enormously admired Clessie's mechanical genius, his flair for the spectacular, and his ability to charm a group. W. G. used to relate with relish how foolish his friends in New York thought him to be for investing so much money over so long a time in a business that showed no financial results to speak of."[37]

Crucially, "in spite of occasional tiffs, W. G. and Clessie Cummins continued to function as a remarkably complementary team… John Niven [briefly number two under Clessie in the early thirties] said it best: 'W. G. and Clessie never weakened at the same time.'"[38] At least twice, W. G. wanted to shutter the business: late in 1927, but the Pennsylvania Railroad miraculously ordered three locomotives; and late in1929, after the October crash of the stock market, but Clessie put a U engine in a five-year-old Packard car, drove to the New York City auto show, and in January 1930 broadly demonstrated the fuel efficiency of his product. Four times in the late 1920s, Clessie tried to sell the business, but W. G. blocked his way and "prevailed on keeping Cummins Engine in Columbus for what it might someday do for the town."[39]

Then there was Linnie. Her brother, W. G., and Clessie might "blow hot and then cold" at different times, but never she. Cummins Engine was her memorial to that beloved, departed brother, Joe, who had died so tragically in that swimming accident in 1900.

2

A Foundation in Faith

Miller was an unshakeable Christian throughout his life. He was also devoutly proud of where he had come from. Drawing on his Judeo-Christian upbringing in Columbus, Miller often cited the book of Isaiah, chapter 51: "'Look to the rock from which you are hewn and to the quarry from which you are digged'—it's only through a profound acquaintance with the follies and achievements of those who have preceded you that you can discover your own inherited weaknesses."[1] Predicated on his Greco-Roman studies in college, he explained, "The only really valid definition of patriotism I've ever found came out of Tacitus: 'Praiseworthy competition with one's ancestors'! I may not have all their powers, but am I knocking myself out to the extent those fellows did? There's where the drive comes from."[2]

While the family may be most known for founding Cummins Engine Company, their identity was really formed around faith. J. Irwin Miller's grandfathers, Z. T. Sweeney and John Chapman Miller, were both ministers with the Christian Church (Disciples of Christ). And Z. T. had a strong hand in creating Christian Theological Seminary in Indianapolis—an extraordinary accomplishment that provides rich testament about his forebears.

As the nineteenth century ended and the twentieth century started, Miller's forebears, as leaders of the Christian Church (Disciples of Christ)—both lay and professional—were intently interested in producing a strong flow of new ministers, particularly from Disciples' colleges. Yet their path proved profoundly difficult (as documented in

Christian Theological Seminary, Indianapolis, written by Keith Watkins and published in 2001).[3]

The focus of their energy was Indianapolis's Butler University, where Miller's ancestors typically had attended college. Paternal grandfather, John Chapman Miller, Indianapolis minister, in 1890 unsuccessfully tried to add five people to the Butler University faculty, "two of them in Bible studies."[4] Great grandfather Joseph I. Irwin in 1898 pledged $25,000 (of a $100,000 goal) to endow the Bible College of Indiana. But, unfortunately it closed in 1902.[5]

By the time Irwin Miller was a boy, great uncle W. G. and maternal grandfather, Z. T. Sweeney, both on the board of directors of Butler, were trying "to bring wealthy committed Disciples from around the nation to support ... the central school they intended to create... at Butler."[6] W. G. Irwin provided in 1919 a salary of $4,000 per annum to Frederick D. Kershner, to create a central training school for the Disciples of Christ,[7] a college at Butler.

The university's directors appointed a committee of five to consider the proposal (including Z. T. Sweeney and Hugh T. Miller, "a strategic choice as chair... because he was the son of a Disciples minister and longtime Butler trustee John Chapman Miller, Z. T. Sweeney's son-in-law and W. G. Irwin's business partner").[8] In June of 1920, the committee proposed a school—a graduate school, primarily to be part of Butler, rather than independent.[9]

The following year, the Christian Foundation was organized with a ten-man board of "prominent Disciples," including W. G. Irwin, and in 1922, the Butler Foundation was established with W. G. Irwin named as its president.[10]

When his protégé, Kershner, threatened to leave for another Disciples school, W. G. increased his efforts "to create the 'Greater Butler' and to relocate to a new campus on the north side of Indianapolis." He and his sister, Linnie, promised a challenge gift of $300,000 to Butler on the basis the university raised another $700,000, for a total of $1 million—but W. G. and Linnie ended up giving $700,000, prompting one trustee to comment in 1924 that their money "was only a small part of their gift because Mr. Irwin is giving of his time, day after day, in helping formulate all the plans."

At last, in 1925, W. G. and Kershner created Butler's new college of religion. Still, "it was part of the university's program."[11] The graduate school of the college of religion was officially acknowledged in a convocation on December 31, 1925, the sermon delivered by Z. T. Sweeney (who would die the next year).

Against a backdrop of the Roaring Twenties, Butler University in its entirety (including the College of Religion) was moved to a new campus north of the city. Additionally, it built a new facility for its basketball program (Hinkle Fieldhouse). But even with W. G. donating another $1 million, Butler "gets in financial trouble." And Walter S. Athearn (who came from Brown University) "is hand-selected by W. G. to lead the University back into solvency and respectability."[12]

Watkins relates, however, that "Athearn's reforms were not enough to correct the problem. W. G. and his sister, Linnie, made up the difference in some years contributing as much as a fourth of the university's budget. Butler's board was increasingly dismayed by the financial crisis... even Irwin became convinced that Athearn's administration had failed.

Furthermore, W. G.'s ability to provide what seemed to be unlimited financial backing was being affected by the costs of his partnership with Clessie Cummins to develop a marketable diesel engine."[13]

Now canny patriarch of the family, W. G. was deriving most of his income (salary and dividends) from the bank and the Union Starch and Refining Company during the thirties.[14] But the drain of Cummins Engine and the College of Religion had to be of concern and cause his moods toward them to rise and fall.

By early 1935, W. G. wanted even greater separation between the college and the university, and, indeed, the next year the family seemed almost inclined to shift its allegiance to a Disciples' university in Oklahoma [Phillips] "unless the Board of Butler would meet their requirements."[15] Fortunately, the years leading up to World War II saw enrollment at the college nearly double, rising from 66 in the 1938/39 academic year to 119 in 1941/42, just before the start of the war.

"Finally," Watkins writes, "the dream of creating a graduate school for Disciples seemed to be reaching its fulfillment. The institutional connections had been negotiated, the financial undergirding assured, and a new building occupied... Instead of going east to Yale... people could come to the School of Religion at Butler University."[16] "Although W. G. Irwin was now past seventy years of age, he exercised power in all aspects of the seminary's life..."[17]

With money now available, Kershner and W. G. in 1942 constructed a separate building for the Seminary, which was called the "School" of Religion, rather than the "College" of Religion, in view of its having a graduate program.[18]

In reality, though, the Irwin-Sweeney-Miller family did not have much to show for the efforts of W. G. and his sister, Linnie (both of whom would die three months apart less than two years later). Their investment of several million dollars of money and thirty-some years of time in the Disciples' seminary had produced only a single building of a simple Georgian design with a room called a "chapel" (albeit the "Sweeney" chapel), set on a campus of a university whose board, at this point, could discontinue its existence whenever it wished.

Yet, it appears that, as deeply devout Christians, they took satisfaction from what they had achieved and believed the work they'd begun would not only please God but be completed by succeeding generations: legal separation of Christian Theological Seminary from Butler, construction of its own physically-remote campus and erection of a free-standing chapel designed by a renowned architect. In this regard, W. G. and Linnie were "cathedral builders", doing all they could in this life to please God, believing they would watch their work completed the next life in the presence of God.

In fact, their grand nephew and grandson, respectively, J. Irwin Miller, would realize their dreams for the Seminary. It seems no two ancestors had the influence on forming Miller's character as W. G. and Linnie. Their courage and vision were seared into his psyche, and prepared him for the challenge -- almost half a century later -- of saving the engine company, which would not boom until after his death.

Growing up in Columbus probably wasn't much fun for Miller, but it set the stage for a remarkable life. "Little Irwin, left-handed to begin with, stuttered miserably and showed no talent at all for a role of leadership in his first ten grades at Columbus public schools."[19] He likely was self-conscious, if not embarrassed, living in one of the town's largest houses (certainly its most ornate, throwing in the Italianate garden), owned by the wealthiest (or close to it) family that had three or four servants.

Miller recalled that he wore short pants through grade school (weather permitting) and that his peers "thought I was a goody-goody. I had only three friends growing up—Ray Eddy [two years younger], who lived in the same block [his dad was a master carpenter], Ben Kroot, [who] lived one block north [son of a local scrap yard owner], and Charlie Cavanagh [orphan, no parents], [who] cleaned spittoons at the Elks Club."[20]

Clessie Cummins, family chauffeur and then co-owner of the engine company with W. G. and his sister, Linnie Sweeney, said in his autobiography that he was

> the boy's closest companion during his childhood and growth to maturity. Despite the score of year's difference in our ages, I sometimes gave the impression of being an overgrown child. Young Irwin Miller and I were to romp away many hours together.

> Because of the family's reluctance to expose him to the companionship of other youngsters in the community, he had no opportunity to experience what I would consider to be a normal childhood. Like his Great Uncle before him [W. G.], young Miller grew up in a household dominated by women.

> So the lad delighted in freeing up his pent up aggressions during his many sessions of horseplay he engaged in with me. I became a means of emotional release as well

as a companion. I gradually came to regard him as a combination of brother and son.[21]

Miller recalled that he "got Cs and Es in grade school, not quite as good as Clementine [his sister]."[22] One teacher really impressed him, though: "Mrs. Condo, probably the best Latin teacher the world ever saw—and the scariest—but as I continued Latin for eight more years, I never met another student who had been given as good a preparation as I received [in Columbus]."[23]

Curiously, Miller never learned to speak a modern language fluently, other than his native English, though his father, Hugh, spoke perfect French, Spanish, and German.[24] However, his aunt Elsie and mother, Nettie, taught Clementine and him to play the violin.

The mansion at 608 Fifth Street must have given Miller a special sense of security, when he was inside. Later in life, he wrote, "My favorite room was always the one at the top of the tower, overlooking Fifth Street. It was the highest room in the house, and it opened onto the attic which had many interesting corridors and closets, and on rainy days this is where I and my friends spent most of our time playing."[25]

It is likely, too, that Miller (and his sister) learned to enjoy the three-times-a-day "get-togethers" with the grown-ups at the dinner table, where everything got talked out.

Perhaps, though, "the best part of [his] childhood came in the annual migration to the remote summer home on Lake Rousseau [in Canada] where the whole family escaped the responsibilities of Columbus."[26]

In the tenth grade, Miller was sent away to Taft, a boys' boarding school in Watertown, Connecticut, because his family was concerned about the quality of the education at Columbus High School.[27] No doubt they were emboldened by the good experience Clementine had had at Emma Willard, a girls' boarding school, in Troy, New York. Per family lore, during the interview with Miller, his mother, Nettie, asked the headmaster, Horace Dutton Taft, "Why should I entrust my son to you?" She was hooked when he replied, "Almost anyone other than their mother would be better."[28]

"Irwin makes a fine beginning," attaining an 83 percent average in his first semester in the fall of 1923, wrote the headmaster, but he added, "My only concern is that he is not enjoying life. He is shy and retiring and does not enter into things much."[29] As though oblivious to the administration, Miller eschewed athletics and extracurricular pursuits, focused on his studies, grinding out honors marks in all of his courses and graduating cum laude (top 10 percent). His average reached 89 percent in his last semester in the spring of 1927,[30] and to make his parents even more proud, the headmaster on wrote June 17, 1927 that "Irwin has something better than scholastic ability and achievement. He has a character of pure gold. I expect to hear fine things from him."[31]

THE TAFT SCHOOL,
WATERTOWN,
CONNECTICUT.

June 17, 1927.

My dear Mrs. Miller:

I enclose Irwin's final report.
I need hardly repeat what I said to you when you were
here. Irwin has had an extraordinary record. He has
the medal in Mathematics, and Mr. Weld says that he
has done as good work for him as any pupil Mr. Weld ever
had. This is high praise. Of course, he has Honors in
every study.

Irwin has something better than
scholastic ability and achievement. He has a character
of pure gold. I expect to hear fine things from him all
along the line, and I am very glad that we can count
upon him as an old boy.

Sincerely yours,

Horace D. Taft

Mrs. Hugh Th. Miller.

This letter from Taft boarding school's headmaster
surely made Miller's parents proud.
Provided by the Indiana Historical Society

3

On-the-Job Training

Miller's boarding school, Taft, was a feeder school for Yale. Thus he probably didn't give a whole lot of thought to moving on to New Haven. Years later, Miller wrote, "When I attended Yale College, it was academically exciting but socially uninvolved, remarkable, considering that my last two years were the first and worst Depression years."[1] It's a rare, somewhat disingenuous comment, because Miller then was driving around campus in a new LaSalle automobile given him by "Unc" in his junior year.

As an undergraduate at Yale, Miller performed well academically but remained in what he called an "adolescent fog."[2] A liberal arts student, he took a broad array of courses, including math, physics, and English, but majored in Latin and minored in Greek.

He did neither sports nor extracurriculars. He wasn't interested much, evidently, in making lots of new friends. He roomed for three years with a former classmate from Taft, Maynard Mack, and had no use for "secret societies" (e.g., Skull and Bones—Yale's fraternities, if you will), and they likely didn't see much in him.[3] Miller was engrossed in his course work, and it paid off: in 1931, he graduated Phi Beta Kappa and magna cum laude.

Upon graduation, Miller went to Oxford University's Balliol College to get a master's degree in the liberal arts. Again, he lived with a former classmate from Taft, Seymour Dribben. At Oxford, he began to loosen up. He played violin in the symphony, rowed with the crew, went to parties, and traveled through Europe on vacation, usually with Dribben (and once with Unc in 1931).[4]

In a letter home the end of the second (and last) year, Miller wrote (as he frequently did), "The amount of work I have done has not been more than one-sixth what I did in my laziest days at New Haven,"[5] not providing Unc a lot of incentive to send his great-nephew back for a third year.

This sketch of a steam locomotive, found on the inside cover of a notebook Miller used at Oxford, attests to his skill at drawing and his thoughts of home.
Provided by the Indiana Historical Society

No doubt influenced by his great-uncle W. G., when Miller graduated, he decided on a career in business rather than teaching or preaching.[6] But Harvard Business School, then just getting started, was ruled out as a stepping-stone: "Business could not be taught," proclaimed W. G.[7] So where to place the shy classics major? Upon his return from Oxford to Indiana in the summer of 1933, aged twenty-four, Miller was ready to stake his claim.

Irwin Union Bank, the strongest of the family's businesses, likely did not seem suitable, because it had solid management, including W. G. and Miller's father, Hugh. Union Starch and Refining, a corn products producer 78 percent owned by the family, Miller later recalled, was "very profitable right through the Depression… and [had] accumulated cash… invested primarily in common stocks and personally managed by W. G. [amounting to] more than $20 million at the time of my return [from England]." But its location (Granite City, Illinois) probably turned Miller off.[8]

Cummins Engine, though losing money every year since its founding in 1919, appeared finally by 1934 to have a viable product for a commercial truck (the H engine). While Miller was still attending Oxford, Cummins Engine began putting out a product the family was proud of. "When a Cummins engine ran," recalled Miller, "it was superb and better than anyone else's... There were forty-some competitors and none of them any good either... We worked night and day to improve and fought one disaster after another... A Caterpillar official once said, 'They're not engineers at Cummins... they don't have sense when to give up.'"[9]

Clessie's debut of the incredibly fuel-efficient U engine at the 1930 New York City auto show was groundbreaking, but he had only built the one engine. Its successor, the H truck engine, however, debuted in 1932 to a "firm and successful introduction"—Clessie was heeding the advice of no less than Henry Ford (Clessie knew all the auto executives) to "consider only trucks, [warning] 'When you make a mistake with a new car engine you instantly have thousands to fix, but with a truck engine, your production will start out small and the number to service manageable,' [so] trucks were the target market."[10] And in 1934, "We all agreed to abandon two-cycle research," Clessie wrote, in order to focus on four-cycle research.[11]

But Cummins also had a capable business manager in John Niven, borrowed in early 1930 from the family's fourth business, Purity Stores, to help Clessie on the commercial side as general manager. So no room for Miller there.[12] And, lastly, there was Purity Stores itself. Purity (patterned after Piggly Wiggly, America's first grocery chain) operated one-hundred-odd supermarkets in California. It was owned 50 percent by W. G. and 50 percent by its two young managers, Niven and Ivan Heddon, protégés of W. G. years earlier when W. G. ran Stokley-Van Camp, a vegetable packer located in Indianapolis.[13]

However, within weeks of Miller's return to the United States, Heddon died unexpectedly, "forcing Niven to return to San Francisco on short notice" to run Purity, and the family decided to send Miller with Niven "and spend the rest of the year in various positions with

Purity, learning the nitty-gritty of business… a useful training ground for management of Cummins" (or so wrote the authors of *The Engine That Could*).[14]

Miller later recalled, "I worked in the back room of stores, sorting potatoes. I waited on the counter. I lived in boardinghouses. John Niven moved me around."[15]

Miller's son Will believes his forebears had a hidden agenda for his dad: a blue-collar antidote to the two fey years in Oxford, punting on the Thames and fiddling in the salons.[16]

Heddon's death, necessitating Niven's return to the West Coast, thus opened up the general manager job at the engine company in mid-1934. It was yet another instance of fate affecting the Irwin-Sweeney-Miller clan—like Clessie starting Mr. Irwin's Packard, Uncle Joe dying in the river accident, and the father, Hugh, contracting tuberculosis.

But Cummins was still really being run by W. G. and Clessie. Though new to engine manufacturing, Niven, in nearly four years as general manager (number two to Clessie), had been an important, stabilizing influence, especially in helping open a West Coast market for truck engines (using Purity as a "beta site").[17] With Niven gone, important decisions had to be made by W. G. and/or Clessie.

But W. G. was a behind-the-scenes player at Cummins throughout the 1930s. "Miller [recalled] with chagrin the regular trips that he and Clessie made to W. G.'s office, where they would present big plans… [W. G.] wouldn't look up. He would go on signing papers or doing whatever he was doing, while I was making my big speech. Then, he'd say, 'How much do you want? I'm busy.' Miller would name the amount and leave with check in hand, frustrated by his limited authority."[18]

Meanwhile, Clessie's relationship with the engine company began to fracture. He had a heavy travel schedule. He was still devoting a good deal of time to racing Cummins-powered cars but also would sometimes just disappear to ride his boat on the Ohio River. Then, starting in 1937, he began to have serious health problems.[19]

Also, there were vacations. W. G. went north to Canada each summer. Clessie went south to Florida each winter.

In addition to often physically being out of touch, the two owners were living in the past to a large extent. In 1939, twenty years after the founding of the company, W. G. and his sister, Linnie, reminded Clessie of the raison d'être for founding the company. Clessie, in replying, repeated what they'd originally agreed to: "The primary reason [to start CECo] was to create a training school for the community... It has never been [our] intention to build up a gigantic industry or become the 'Ford' of the diesel engine field... The problem of how large we should grow is going to be... the most difficult to solve... None of us wants to see the business grow to the point where... a great influx of help has to be brought in, resulting in sooner or later a big layoff with the resulting misery and upsetting of the entire community."[20]

Besides tending to manage from a distance and regarding the engine company as a vocational school, the owners during the thirties were at odds over what markets to pursue, even as the company, per se, was heading in a different direction! W. G. emphatically told Clessie in 1934, "You're going into the railroad business!"[21] And in 1939, W. G. advised Clessie to look into making diesel engines for transatlantic airplanes.[22] For his part, Clessie was hoping to produce A engines for Cord (which, perhaps providentially for CECo, went bankrupt the next year).[23]

Fortunately, despite a good deal of confusion at the top of the company in the decade of the thirties, Cummins Engine Company could not suppress its growth. Between 1929 and 1939, employment soared from fifty to seven hundred.[24] The period which ended March 1937 was the company's first-ever profitable quarter, and 1937 itself was its first-ever profitable year—after seventeen consecutive years of losses.

Sales of diesel-powered trucks were starting to take off in the United States, and Cummins in particular was beginning to benefit from a reputation of reliability and durability due to its workhorse H engine. Where Cummins sold 133 engines in 1933, it shipped 4,745 engines in 1941, "the vast majority of them for use in trucks."[25] The United States entered World War II following the attack on Pearl Harbor.

W. G. and Clessie evidently were in agreement that the young general manager needed help in these circumstances. A key addition was Vincent E. McMullen, hired as works manager in charge of production in April 1935. Though sixty-five years old, "Mr. Mac" brought years of engine-making experience to Columbus.[26] Another example was E. Don Tull, promoted in 1935 from hourly to foreman of critical cylinder-block and connecting-rod lines, with thirty-five employees, and in 1940 to superintendent of the machine shop, with seven hundred employees.[27]

But Miller brought an intangible unity to the company, from top to bottom, that would carry it through decades to come. He apparently didn't just issue orders and sit in his office. Practicing Christian principles driven into him as a child, Miller evidently worked hard at relating to Cummins's employees, personally difficult as it might have been. A visitor taken on a tour of the plant by Miller in 1936 observed, "I didn't get the sense that he was completely in charge of things, but I noticed how many of the men on the line knew him… He'd call these people by their first names and explain the process they went through. He was very relaxed in here."[28]

As for labor unions, the young general manager was on his own—these were new phenomena in America. The Wagner Act, passed by the US Congress in 1935, "guaranteed workers the right to organize freely and required employers to bargain collectively." In the spring of 1937, the CIO (Congress of Industrial Organization) began a recruitment drive at Cummins.[29]

On the evening of May 21, Miller addressed "a large audience of Cummins workers assembled in the high school gymnasium." The authors of *The Engine That Could* wondered

> How could the young manager—new to the company and the industry, a scion of one of Indiana's elite families—appeal to working-class factory men and their families? How could he persuade them to spurn Union promises of higher wages, increased benefits,

and improved job security—especially [during] the Depression?

Rather than sidestep these stark disparities in experience and class, Miller confronted them head-on, and with remarkable candor:

Now, in all this talk, there is one thing at least that is undeniable and that is that I am the last fellow on earth that has any business coming here and talking to you, because, if there has ever been a fellow who has had a soft, easygoing life, it has been me, and I can't have the least idea what it is like to wonder every night when I go home whether I'll have a job when I go back in the morning or whether I will be eating this time next month.

Miller then asked the company's workers to consider the short, terrible history of their company—how Clessie began with a vision but a poor product, how W. G. stayed with him, absorbing loss after financial loss… that neither W. G. nor Clessie had collected a penny of return from the business [apart from Clessie's small salary']… Miller asked the men to consider how we have treated you throughout this period of financial hardship. And now, he asked rhetorically, were some 'gentlemen from Chicago' likely to treat them better?[30]

Miller believed that his employees would be better served under local leadership than under a national union.

The next day, Cummins's employees rejected the CIO's bid. They also turned down a second organizing attempt by the CIO a month later and formed a company union (the Cummins Employees Association, or CEA), which negotiated a one-year contract with the company on July 16.[31]

While the following spring, 1938, the National Labor Relations Board declared the CEA "invalid," a few weeks later, Cummins's workers voted to form another independent union—the Diesel Workers Union—and this time received the sanction of the NLRB.[32]

As the decade of the thirties ended, Miller clearly was having an impact on the family business. As World War II approached, Cummins Engine Company appeared to have quite a bright future. It had been a roller-coaster ride.[33]

4

All Is Fair in Love and War

It had to be a case of "opposites attract." He was six foot two inches; she was just five foot four. He grew up amid great wealth; she, abject poverty. He'd spent ten years in private schools; she, none. He'd attained college and master's degrees; she'd only gone through high school. They both joined Cummins Engine in 1934, but he started at the top; she, at the bottom as a clerk in the purchasing department.

Miller's wife-to-be was born Xenia Ruth Simons in 1917 in Morgantown, Indiana (between Bloomington and Indianapolis). She had three siblings, but they were nine to twelve years older than she was. Their father's first job had been selling silos to farmers in southwest Ohio, including the town of Xenia. "He always liked this town's name, so I got it,"[1] she recalled in a short memoir she prepared in 1999 (then aged eighty-two).

When she was little, Xenia's father ran a small lumber mill and made hickory furniture.

> We were poor, and that was before disaster struck, when I was ten. My father had cosigned a note for a man in Chicago and the man had disappeared... The bank demanded payment which cost my father his business and his home.

> We moved to Colfax, Indiana [between Lafayette and Indianapolis] to try to start another hickory factory... which failed. We lived in a rented house which had one small stove where the fire went out at night and the milk on the table froze in its jars. It was very cold.

The next year... we moved to Columbus... The rent
was $1 per day and we wondered how we were going
to pay it. I went to Garfield School... for three months
in the spring to finish fifth grade. The principal...
recommended me for... a progressive class [where] I
flourished. In one year under a most wonderful teacher,
Miss Elizabeth Harm, I passed the sixth and seventh
grades and most of the eighth.

However, disaster struck again, and we moved to
North Vernon, a railroad town which I hated. The
school officials didn't know where to place me. Then
an opportunity came for my father to go back to
Columbus[2]... where the "Columbus Hickory Chair
Company" was started... It was nip and tuck with no
spare money... Once we had only one can of mother's
canned peaches in the basement to eat. And the nice
grocer... couldn't allow us any more credit. That was
the only time I remember going to bed hungry, but the
next day Dad sold a footstool and we eked through.

Fortuitously, Xenia attended Tabernacle Christian Church, and,
graduating from high school at the depth of the Depression in 1934,
she was offered a loan to take business classes by Nettie Miller (her
future mother-in-law), enabling her to get a job at Irwin Union Bank
for a few months until she was hired by Cummins Engine and placed
in its purchasing department,[3] where she would work for seven years.

By early 1941, "it had become a common sight to see the two
walking together along Fifth Street heading for lunch downtown
or returning to the office where they both worked."[4] At some point,
they sat across from each other at a table, bargaining a new contract
between the company and its Office Committee Union (or OCU),
and a handwritten note presumably passed from Miller to Xenia is
reproduced on the next page.[5]

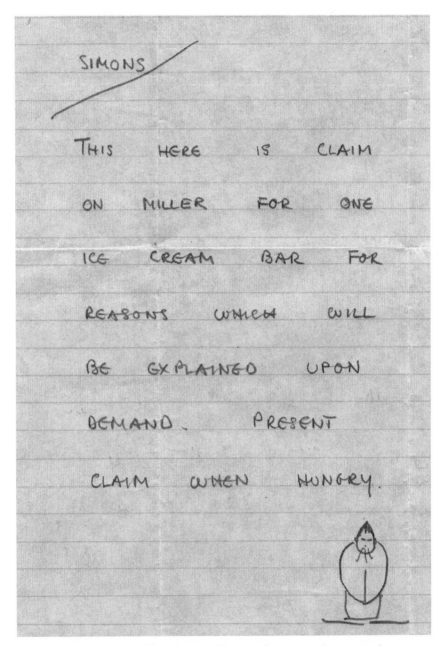

Before going off to war, Miller sent his co-worker — and
future wife — Xenia Simons, this invitation for an ice
cream at Zaharako's in Columbus, Indiana.
Provided by the Indiana Historical Society

Romance is typically hurried along by war, and theirs was no exception. The United States entered World War II on December 7, 1941. In the spring of 1942, Miller, who'd just turned thirty-three, joined the navy. He trained at Quonset Point, Rhode Island, graduating on August 8, second in a class of 750, and was appointed a lieutenant.[6] It is to Miller's everlasting credit that he endured his pre–World World II apprenticeship at the engine company—it likely prepped him for the real combat to come.[7]

They wrote each other daily (except for leaves) until he came home for good in May 1944. In their letters, they referred to each other as "Gramma" and "Grampa":

A letter to Miller, dated October 22, 1942: "Gosh, Grampa, you're nice, and I love you all the time. Do you know how good and wonderful you really are; Granpop? And, Grampa, I hope we can be Mr. and Mrs. Granpop very soon, too. There's not much else I want—Gramma."[8]

And to Xenia, dated November 23, 1942: "I never realized how much love keeps a fellow going. Nothing is too rough or too unpleasant or too dull because you are near me all the time. In return, darling, a fellow can give nothing less than himself—and you have my heart—for keeps—Grampa."[9]

He had just bought her a diamond ring at Tiffany & Co. in New York City for $620[10] and proposed to her. Not taking his advice, she wore her ring in public (in Columbus) and immediately regretted the decision:

> I wish I were a thousand miles away. I wish you had never given me a ring... Now I've put your family on the spot before the whole town... I'm beset with torments and fears. I'm poor—my family and I never have an extra dime—and kinda dumb with no education and I don't know which fork to use and when—and Grampa, that kind wouldn't make a good wife for you.[11]

The material at the Indiana Historical Society contains no mention of his family's feelings on their sole male heir (in two generations) proposing marriage to Miss Simons. We assume they felt he was "marrying down." In any event, none of Miller's family attended the wedding ceremony February 5, 1943, in the chapel of a Christian church in Washington, DC.

"Clessie was Miller's best man and Stella [Clessie's wife][12] stood by Xenia's side… [The family] were chagrined for a while at the suddenness of what happened. However, W. G. visited the newlyweds in their small Virginia apartment before Irwin left for his ship."[13]

We suppose that Miller saw in Xenia a pert, puckish, bright young woman badly wanting to improve her situation. Despite his growing up at 608 Fifth Street, he realized he, too, was only a couple of generations removed from "tilling the soil."

Mainly, though, he was a staunch egalitarian. Writing Xenia just before he left Cummins Engine for the navy, he mused about "the spirit that has made it possible for us to do a very great deal with very little [at Cummins Engine]… I believe the spirit will continue to grow because those in authority have been for the most part kind and humble persons with a love for those that work with them. There is no one who understands and feels all this as well as you, my sweet. It is easy to write it to you where it would be near impossible to say it to another."[14] In other words, she was the apotheosis of the people he revered at the engine company.

"The navy had a huge impact on Dad," says his son Will, mainly the exposure to enlisted personnel and people management on a grand scale.[15] While Miller's seagoing days would last less than a year, the lessons he learned about people and organizations would help mold his thinking for the rest of his life.

After Quonset Point, Miller spent several months at a desk job in Washington, DC, and was then assigned to duty on March 1943 on a ship nearly constructed. Launched May 1943, at the New York

Shipbuilding Corporation yard in Brooklyn, the *Langley* was a light, fast aircraft carrier of the Independence class.[16] She then was up-fitted at the Philadelphia Naval Shipyard, taken to Trinidad on a shakedown cruise, and, after last-minute touches, departed for war in the Pacific in late fall,[17] allowing Miller a short leave in Columbus to say farewell to his wife, Xenia, by then pregnant with the first of their five children— Margaret, born in December.

Presciently, regarding a visit to Cummins Engine while home, he wrote his sister, Clementine: "To my delight, the union and office committee [referring to the DWU and OCU] are not only still in existence, but flourishing."[18] The navy had exposed Miller to a totally different organizational arrangement that would inform, and indeed confirm, his ideas on people for the rest of his life.

Miller had already had years of experience dealing with labor-management issues. According to his son Will, Miller "always had greater respect for the little guy than the front-line manager."[19] Will says his father just assumed the hourly was right.[20]

In Miller's view, there were problems up and down the *Langley's* organization. Above him, the "regular officers [or Annapolis graduates]," he wrote his wife, "want the Admirals to 'cater' to them, but they do not want to have to 'cater' to the men under them. Like most everybody else, they believe in two forms of society—democracy from me on up, and autocracy from me on down. That seems like the ideal solution to the ills of the world," he told Xenia, tongue in cheek. "I guess they have me figured out for an irresponsible Bolshevik."[21]

A larger problem, in Miller's view, was the enlisted rank, whose experience, skills, and motivation officers often underrated. An even bigger matter, however, was that the US services in World War II were segregated.

Growing up in privilege, Miller's biggest exposure to black people consisted of the maids at 608 Fifth Street. African Americans made up less than 1 percent of the population of Columbus in the forties. The navy would give him an "immersion course" about the plight of black people that would be seared into his psyche and inform and affect his words and deeds the rest of his life.

In a letter that October to his folks, he rapped out his observations on his portable Remington typewriter (remarkably, free of errors):

> The colored boys continue to surprise me. I would have thought that they would have submitted to Navy discipline more easily than the independent white boys. This is not so. Maybe one reason is that the white boys know they have a future ahead of them in the Navy, while the colored boys know that no matter how they behave they will never get any other job than that of serving officers. Thus they apparently do not care, and would just as soon be in the brig as sit it out… the colored boys are booted around and treated as the white boys would never be, and quite possibly are showing some understandable resentment. I am trying to help improve the situation—with so far no results.

Miller's concern and compassion for blacks was evident to his fellow officers. In early November, during the shakedown cruise before leaving for combat, Miller wrote his wife ("Mama," he called her): "The Commander decided to give me the problem children—the mess cooks and the colored boys… about a hundred and twenty men," in addition to his other duties.[22] In December, evidently prior to sailing from Philadelphia and availing themselves of the local brig, Miller wrote his parents: "We have now got rid of our worst gents and the work and morale is much improved… One of the troubles is… that they don't often get told so, though they always get told when they do something wrong. Also, they are treated as dogs (only not so well)."[23]

Back in Indiana, meantime, Xenia, now in her eighth month of pregnancy and living at 608 Fifth Street, continued to endure difficulties with her in-laws. She wrote on November 5, "Your folks are perfectly wonderful... and want me to stay here... but I find it so different from any place I've ever lived before... I'm always afraid I'm not polite enough—don't stand up when I should—not report my movements—don't say the right thing at the right time. I've never had the opportunity to learn much of the art of gracious living, Grampa, and it doesn't come naturally and smoothly." She would move into a small apartment before the baby was born.[24] In December 1943, with Miller still away at war, Xenia gave birth to their first child, Margaret.

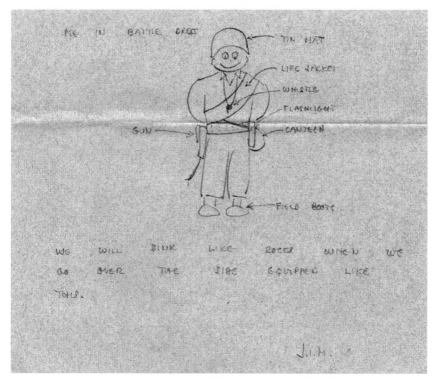

From an aircraft carrier in the Pacific in early 1944, Miller mailed his new wife, Xenia, a sketch of himself in combat gear.
Provided by the Indiana Historical Society

That same month, Miller got news that his great-uncle, W. G. Irwin, had died. Apparently, after yet another business dispute between him and Clessie, Clessie sent a letter of resignation to W. G., who "was quite upset by the letter," according to Miller's mother, Nettie. Nettie later drove W. G. to a meeting at the Indiana National Bank in Indianapolis, where he had a heart attack and died in the lobby. Clessie subsequently withdrew his resignation.[25]

Miller immediately applied for seven months' inactive duty. He wrote his parents, "I shall give as reasons that active heads must be selected for three organizations [Union Starch, bank, and engine company] all more or less connected with the war effort... [But] I have requested return to the ship—to show them that I am not trying to get out of anything and actually do want to return to it."[26]

Writing his wife, Xenia, from his ship in the Pacific after learning about W. G.'s death in December 1943, Miller professed, "Uncle's standards and ideals are mine... I can't tell you how much I loved him, Mamaw, because the words won't come."[27] To his folks, a week later, he recounted, "Uncle was such a shy person... all the talk about the powerful banker and great manufacturer didn't seem like Uncle to me. The Uncle I remember so vividly is the Uncle whose face was lit up with enthusiasm about something... maybe it was the church, or maybe it was some little kid he had met on the street."[28]

Miller's petition, however, was almost immediately denied,[29] and simultaneously, the *Langley* proceeded to the Pacific and final training at Pearl Harbor before sailing to war.

Miller's exact whereabouts the first few months of 1944 are imprecise (for obvious reasons, naval personnel were under strict orders not to disclose their locations, and if censors caught violators, punishment was severe). He wrote his sister, "I live in real luxury with [a] room boy to make up the room, stow loose gear, and shine shoes every day. We have good food, now and then curried shrimp or steak and French fried onions, or as today, good Creole omelet and we have made a port at fairly frequent intervals. As we daily say 'it's a hard war'... No one has a goal of winning of the war, or beating of Japan for these aren't things to keep men's spirits going or to make the time pass, or to survive. The goal is always 'this time next week we'll be in "so and so" and I know a good beer joint there' or 'maybe in three months we'll go into dry-dock and have every night liberty.'"[30] And on January 9, 1944, he wrote his parents, saying about his sister, Clementine, who served in the Red Cross in Italy near the front line, "I am somewhat jealous of her, for she is certainly far more a part of the war than we are living in our comfortable room, eating good chow, and basking [on] the beach every now and then."[31]

Matters militarily, however, got serious for Miller when the *Langley* ("one of thirteen aircraft carriers which bore the brunt of the Pacific Air-Sea Offensive," per the magazine *SEAPOWER*),[32] sortied from Pearl Harbor on January 19, 1944, heading for the Marshalls, and arriving on April 30, 1944). Not only was there the ever-present threat that Japanese torpedoes or bombs could find their way through the *Langley*'s hull to thousands of gallons of aviation fuel and sink the ship but it also is evident that Miller and his shipmates did come under direct attack[33]— strafings from Japanese Zeroes. "Don't think I didn't get scared," he wrote Clementine. "Luckily I had a battle station that kept me too busy to do much thinking about myself."[34]

As the *Langley* encountered its first combat, Miller, denied temporary leave, had to be concerned about events back home. He was worried about the engine company. On January 9, 1944, he wrote Xenia that "Clessie [Cummins] is a fine loyal, warm-hearted guy and about the best friend I have, [but] he is sick and confused." He wanted to be with Xenia and the baby.

Then in February of 1944, Miller learned of the death of his grandmother Linnie. Encouraged by his commanding officer, W. M. Dillon, Miller again requested leave and this time received ninety days' inactive duty beginning on May 12, 1944.[35] He was back home on May 21!

In leaving the *Langley* for good, Miller had to be satisfied with his accomplishment. His skipper Dillon wrote him, "You made the effort and performed a man's job in my command. As a matter of fact, I took considerable pride in your qualifications as an Officer of the Deck— underway at sea in formation. I had no better Officer of the Deck."[36]

Importantly, active duty at sea during wartime boosted Miller's confidence in average (i.e., blue collar) people. Shortly before leaving the *Langley* the last time on March 16, 1944) he wrote Xenia, "We have such a wonderful chance in Columbus in the Engine Company. We have the chance to see whether or not a business organization cannot be organized and run in a manner that permits a person in it a personal dignity, voice in its operation proportionate to his ability to contribute, and a chance to work at work that is satisfying and to gain recognition for work well done."[37]

Above all, naval experience boosted his self-confidence. "For the first time, I was judged solely on my own merits," said Miller. "It was very important to me to make good [in the Navy]… I always felt there was a cloud hanging over my head in Columbus—the thought that I wasn't exactly the people's choice, and that I have been inserted in the job."[38]

Incredibly, Miller and Xenia, in addition to writing to each other daily, saved all their correspondence. Imagine Miller taking off from the *Langley* with all of her letters stowed in his luggage!

5

The Changing of the Guard

When Miller returned from the front lines in 1944, he found that things at the engine company were worse than he'd feared—it would be a great test of character and reveal what sort of leader he had become. First, he wrote the Secretary of the Navy, James V. Forrestal, asking for a permanent discharge:

> Cummins employs 1800 persons, manufactures diesel engines for the Army and Navy, has annual gross sales of $26 million and is engaged solely in military production… Mr. Cummins, the President, is in poor health and is unable to play an active part in the business. Mr. McMullen, appointed General Manager upon my departure, is 65 and desirous of retirement. The Bank is anxious over our present management situation.[1]

It worked, and in July of 1944, his resignation was accepted in a letter signed by Forrestal.

From a manufacturing standpoint, Cummins was still innovating. Before the war, the company was focused mostly on over-the-road trucks with its H engine (of which twenty-thousand had been built by this time).[2] After much trial and error, Clessie and his engineers had decided that the H would be the company's workhorse. But it needed to be bigger and more powerful: six cylinders, not four; in-line configuration, not *V*; four cycle, not two (with supercharger optional). Embodying these criteria, the NH (for New H) debuted in 1945 as the war ended and, incorporating in 1951 the PT injector technology, which Clessie had invented and patented way back in 1921, powered the company for nearly four decades, accounting for some 78 percent of revenues as late as 1980![3]

But toward the end of W. G.'s life, things became worse between Clessie and him. As Miller recalls, "Clessie grew increasingly irritated as he became older that W. G. still treated him as a dependent son—and not as an equal ... W. G., however, remained convinced that CLC could not handle his personal finances and that unless he was kept heavily in common stock and tight on cash, he would never accumulate any substance." Where at the foundation of the company Clessie owned 50 percent and W. G. and Linnie together owned 50 percent, Clessie quickly slipped into a status of minority shareholder as he impulsively sold shares to raise cash for his family... W. G. used to be shocked by CLC's "extravagances" in pursuing his personal hobbies of cameras, guns, and more.

W. G. (and the ladies of the household) also were shocked at CLC's "neglect" of family responsibilities and had considerable sympathy for each of his wives. A further strain on the relationship was their mutual friendship with John Niven. While W. G. treated Niven as an equal in money matters, Clessie was never able to receive the same respect.[4]

The fat finally fell in the fire over a dispute concerning the Oil Engine Development Company. The OEDC had been formed in 1922 by Clessie and W. G.—with the same ownership percentages as Cummins Engine—to conduct research for its parent company, secure patents, and receive royalties.[5] But the company had never been used. So in November 1941, as W. G. was turning seventy-five and tidying up his estate, he decided to merge OEDC with the engine company, giving one hundred shares of Cummins stock to Clessie and one hundred to his sister and himself.

Clessie, however, wanted cash for his OEDC stock—$250,000 ($50,000 per year for five years).[6] "In the year and a half that followed the merger between Cummins and OEDC, Clessie Cummins became increasingly upset with its outcome. He felt trapped... He brooded...

[As he saw things,] his fate was decided 'by star chamber methods.' It was then that he sent the letter of resignation and W. G. had the heart attack. Upon hearing of W. G.'s death, Clessie immediately withdrew his resignation."[7]

After learning of his great-uncle's death while away, Miller types Xenia a five-page, single-spaced letter, where, not until the fourth page, he writes this:

> Don't mention it to the folks, for they haven't mentioned anything about Clessie, but I got a letter from Clessie that was mighty nice, and in it he sort of pledged himself to do what he could to help in the present situation. I hope he doesn't feel that his letter had anything to do with Uncle's going. Clessie used to get that way from time to time, and Uncle was familiar with it, and I'm sure that, while it concerned him, it gave him no serious shock.
>
> You have to believe in what you know in your heart about people—often in spite of their action. And I know that in his heart Clessie is a fine loyal warm-hearted guy, and about the best friend that I have. He is sick and confused, and this takes an odd form of depression at times, but he has been a friend to me when I needed him, and I think he must need help himself now… It would be tactless and wrong even to mention the subject to the folks now, and I shan't do it. I believe that time works most of these things out about right, when both parties mean well in their hearts, as I believe the case to be here.[8]

Time, though, would not work things out, and Clessie seemed to take less and less interest in the business. After successfully re-petitioning for a leave from the navy, Miller was effectively in charge of Cummins

Engine Company with the title of executive vice president. His father, Hugh T., became chairman (reflecting the family's controlling position), and Clessie left the company for good in late 1944 to go to Florida for a few months and then on to California (retaining the title of president for the time being). Miller had come into his major inheritance.

Within six months of his return to Columbus and a few weeks after Clessie left town, Miller exuded confidence. He wrote his sister, Clementine, on November 17, 1944, "If the war is still going strong… then I will tell the Navy to come get me again. [But] my fear is that the moment I left town, Clessie would start raising hell again."[9] In a subsequent letter to Clementine on June 19, 1946, he noted that Clessie "actually did pay $100,000 for his latest palace in Palo Alto, and has three servants full time, and a fifty foot cruiser."[10]

In the summer of 1946, the engine company split its shares fifty to one in a prologue to a public offering. As a result of this recapitalization, Clessie owned 84,600 common shares, and the Irwin-SweeneyMiller family "strongly urged Clessie to hold on to his common stock … [but] he did not. In fact, he sold 50,000 shares… in 1947 for approximately $1 million… Had he held his 84,600 shares for another twenty years [he died in 1968], Clessie would have earned more than $5 million in dividends alone [and] his shares would have grown to 974,592, worth just over $35 million."[11] In fact, by the end of 1954, he owned just fifty shares.[12]

With money seeming to run through his fingers, it is not surprising that, when his patent for an updated PT fuel system got approved in 1954, he'd come knocking on Miller's door, saying that he'd assigned his patent to the engine company "with the expectation that, maybe sometime before my beard tripped me, you'd get around to working out a royalty agreement."[13]

In a five-page, single-spaced, typewritten letter dated June 29, 1954, Miller took umbrage with Clessie:

> I do not believe that any additional payment should be
> made to you by the Company over and above the salary

of $20,000 per year which you have been receiving for the past eight or nine years since you retired and moved to California... The principal gainers for the whole enterprise of CECo have been you and the community of Columbus, not the family, because the family is now in a somewhat less favorable position that it would have been had there been no CECo, but you are in an Immeasurably better position...I do not feel there are any past debts, moral or legal, as between the two original principal participants in the CECo venture.[14]

Yet a year later (June 21, 1955), Miller and Clessie signed an agreement that gave the inventor $125,000 ($25,000 per year for five years).[15]

Curiously, some forty years later, Miller changed his mind about Clessie. In one of half a dozen interviews he gave the authors of *The Engine That Could* between 1993 and 1996, he said, in a show of his undying loyalty and compassion, that the OEDC episode "is one of the things I regret. I could have played a better role there... I could have gotten into it with all four feet and really done it."[16]

Then continues the company-sponsored history—not attributing the sentiment to Miller, per se, but quite possibly using his comments verbatim:

On all accounts, the [Irwin-SweeneyMiller] family got what it needed... Clessie did not, he needed security... had had six children [at nearly age fifty-three]. He was plagued by a baffling illness... that disabled him at unpredictable intervals. As a result, he was very concerned that soon he might be unable to work... Instead of a stake in the OEDC which Clessie valued in the low five figures—he now had to settle for the limited prospect of gains in the common stock... [which] was still not traded publicly, and had no established market value.

Proportionately, Clessie made the bigger sacrifice by far, and he was ill prepared to do so. He and his family felt, with ample justification, that he had already contributed his health and the best years of his life to the Engine Company.[17]

6

The Man and His Passions

As Miller was taking more control of Cummins Engine Company than he ever had and becoming a figurehead for the family, he was also embarking on a personal journey to strengthen his connection with his faith and passions.

Handed down from his ancestors (particularly his two minister grandfathers) and unaffected by his years at Yale and Oxford, his religious beliefs informed everything Miller did—in private life, in business dealings, and in civic matters. In a convocation address at Yale Divinity School in 1985, Miller said

> I must confess that in my early decades the choice was inherited, relatively unexamined, and hence watery at best. As the years have passed, the inheritance has been converted from the accepted and unexamined to a slowly changed but individually tested commitment and guide … The one treasure given each of us is not money, not power, not even peace. It is rather the years of life allotted to us on this planet.
>
> The test of any life lies not all in "success" as defined and reported and judged by others, but rather in what maximum and constructive use each is able to make of his given talents and abilities in his short life span in this world, a world which is beautiful beyond compare, which is ours to love, to use, and to enjoy. My evolving

Christianity has turned out to be my only reliable guide… first I think because it is counter-intuitive. One's intuition is that one should look out for oneself in a world that seems in so many ways frightening and hostile.

But our intuition is wrong. Over and over one sees that looking out for oneself simply doesn't work… the counter-intuitive "lose one's life" [serving others], comes with all the power of miraculous revelations.[1]

Miller was thoroughly familiar and comfortable with the Bible, which he read (more properly, reread) nearly every day. And he would read it in Greek or Latin or English. The first pastor at North Christian Church, which Miller helped build in the 1960s, would later declare, "He was the most biblically literate layman I have ever known."[2]

Actually, he had been pounding away on the "lose one's life" theme his whole life and would continue to do so as long as he had any breath left. Miller incorporated faith into everything from speeches to memos to personal letters. This is a sampling spanning most of his adult life:

1958: "Consider our Lord's description of the last Judgment. Then the King will say to those at his right hand, come, O blessed of my Father, inherit the Kingdom… For I was hungry, and you gave me food. I was thirsty and you gave me drink. I was a stranger and you welcomed me. Was naked and you clothed me. I was sick and you visited me. I was in prison and you came to me… Truly, I say to you, as you did it to one of the least of these, my brethren, you did it to me."[3]

1962: "The most important institution which can ever exist in this nation is the Church of Jesus Christ… Welcome its parental concern into your lives… Lose yourself in it… In so losing your lives, you will find the courage to confront any difficulty."[4]

1964: "Liberty for each of us is found not at all unless it be found in a dominant sacrificial concern for the liberty of the other fellow, especially the deprived and disadvantaged."[5]

1967: "Our true self-interest is always best sought by seeking equally the true interest of every other man, especially those of least advantage."[6]

1972: "I know of no institution other than Christianity that has steadily for 2000 years stood for equality of all individuals, true love of neighbor, responsibility of the well-off for the disadvantaged."[7]

1976: He closes his talk "with the words of Jesus which once were considered so important as to have been included in each of the four Gospels: 'whoever would save his life will lose it, whoever loses his life for my sake and the Gospel's will save it."[8]

1983: "When I have been most preoccupied with myself, most critical of others, most concerned with material things, or lack of them, those were the times when I was most miserable, and most unsure of myself. When I have been able, as in the words of Christ, 'to lose my life' in concern for another rather than myself, or in a project of worth and value, I have been most productive and always happiest."[9]

1987: "So what is leadership?… The unconscious practice of dealing with those for whom you are responsible and those with whom you work in the way you wish your boss would deal with you, in the way you wish your associates would work with you."[10]

1994: His advice to "late 20th century professing Christians 'Don't play it safe"; "Forget yourselves and your introspective guests"; "Lose your lives in prophetic service and mission to this society which is in peril"; "If we are to be, individually and collectively, examples of Christ in our daily lives, then we must come to grips with the real meaning of 'lose your life for my sake and the gospel's' and ask ourselves if we really believe it— enough to practice it every day."[11]

1995: "Christ emphatically meant us to love those whom instinctively we don't want to love: Enemies, Those who have hurt or insulted us, Those who disgust us, Those who irritate us, Those who oppose us, Those who offended us, Those who have slandered us, Those with whom our secret wish might be to get even.[12]

1997: "Lose yourself in commitment to others, never counting cost."[13]

1998: "'Love your neighbor as yourself is the heart of the Christian message."[14]

Deeply rooted in both his emotions and intelligence, Miller's religious beliefs profoundly shaped everything he did, as we will see, in business, civil rights, politics, philanthropy, family—everything.

Meanwhile, music did not just supplement Miller's religiosity— it suffused his faith. Like reading the Bible, playing the violin was typically a daily occurrence. His son Will asserts that "music was more important to my father than architecture."[15]

Starting with lessons as a boy (his mother, aunt, and sister also were violinists), Miller played his "fiddle" (as he referred to it) until old age. He owned both a 1709 Stradivarius and a 1743 Guarnerius del Gesù (the two instruments appraised for $4 million in 1991).[16] To maintain his technique, Miller practiced faithfully, often using *Music Minus One*, a long-playing orchestral recording less the solo part, which he supplied.[17] And he took with him a violin often on business trips and always on vacation to Canada in summer and to Florida in winter. Doug Eckhart, longtime Cummins pilot, recalls that the instrument contained in a leather case was always the last item boarded on the plane, very gently passed up ("We were told not to use the handle but to cradle the violin like a baby") from copilot to pilot, who sat it on the cabin floor by Miller's feet.[18]

Charles H. Webb Jr., retired dean of the Indiana University School of Music and a close friend of the Millers, recalls, "He was passionate regarding music in terms of what it did for him. It was an extremely important part of his life." Webb remembers several joyous evenings at their home, 2760 Highland Way, with Miller playing on his violin Handel's G-Minor Sonata and Webb doing the orchestra's part on a Steinway piano. Webb, though, emphasizes that Miller was an "amateur" as a player. "He knew what he could do and stuck to it, never putting on airs. He wouldn't do Mendelssohn or Tchaikovsky, for example."[19]

If as Webb indicates that Miller's violin playing was of an amateur grade, his knowledge and understanding of music was on a professional level, it seems. He once wrote about a G-major symphony of Hayden where "in the middle of the theme of the slow movements there is an inner B natural played by the English horn or the bassoon... I heard Toscanini and the NBC play this and was (and still am) ravished by the lifting out this single note with delicate emphasis to bring to vivid life Hayden's humanity and his genius for expressing himself."[20]

According to his son Will, Bach was his dad's favorite composer.[21] Miller once wrote the following:

> My own choice of work of western art to be saved at the Holocaust… is the final chorus of [Bach's] St. Matthew's Passion, and in fact it is this penultimate chord of that chorus that cannot be described in words. If that were possible, of course, we wouldn't need the music… The whole work moves inexorably toward forcing the listener to grasp not just in his mind but in his heart that God came onto this planet offering an overwhelming example of love, which was too much for man to take. So they killed the God of love.

> The penultimate chord [is] the realization by means of music of what we have done, and repeatedly still do. A very cultivated Jew, for whom this was a work he felt he had to hear every year, once said to a friend of mine in considerable sorrow that he could not hear it again. Each time, he said, he had to remind himself that he did not believe the story and the message. This, with the passage of time, was even getting too hard for him to sustain.

The Gospel, concluded Miller, "cannot be expressed by words alone."[22] We would assume that Miller would agree with John Eliot Gardiner, who writes in his fine, new biography *Bach: Music in the Castle of Heaven* that the composer's essential promise was "to make a good fist of life, and to face death courageously, joyously even, with hope and faith."[23]

Bach, Miller once explained

> was one of the Christian Church's great theologians, this is often missed. The cantatas, the passions, and

the Mass are generally esteemed in music of the greatest quality. But there is much more here—there is a Christian insight, a point of view, even a Christian revelation, which ranks with the contributions of the greatest church fathers. This is not to be found only in the words of these works. Words alone have never been adequate to encompass the Gospel. It is in a penetrating understanding of Bach, in the meaning behind the words which is revealed in Bach's music that we can finally realize the enormity of his contribution.[24]

7

An Icon of Architecture Is Born

In 1961, Miller wrote, "It is probably true that none of the arts has any greater influence on the tastes and dispositions of men than the architecture with which they are constantly surrounded."[1]

Miller was entranced with architecture. It may not have ranked up there with music but far surpassed art, according to his son Will.[2] It is not totally clear where this interest came from, but his graduate studies at Oxford seem to have disposed him to an architectural sensitivity. He recalled, "In my whole life I know of no more powerful influence than the daily walk from my college to the river and back, past Jesus College, down High Street, through Christ Church, Tom Quad, and the long walk—in every season, in every kind of weather."[3]

Miller went on:

> The architect has a task which is both more difficult and more rewarding than that of other artists. Like them has the thing he wants to say which he wants to achieve. Unlike them, he also has a client, who wants to speak and achieve through the proposed structure, and who looks to the architect to say for him what he cannot say for himself.

> Finally, each structure has a stated purpose as well. That purpose may be anything from an efficient kitchen to a religious sanctuary. But the architect must achieve the purpose or he has accomplished nothing.

Great architecture is, therefore, a triple achievement. It is the solving of a concrete problem, it is the free expression of the architect himself, and it is an inspired and intuitive expression of his client. At its best architecture partakes of immortality, giving joy and excitement to the present, and perpetual challenge to the future.[4]

Quite by accident, Miller, in fact, introduced modern architecture to Columbus, Indiana. A couple of years after he started work at the engine company and before he headed off to war, the congregation of his church, Tabernacle Christian (located where the library now stands), decided to build a new structure and commissioned Edmund Beaman Gilchrist from Philadelphia, who proposed a quite traditional design but was stricken with a nervous breakdown and had to quit. In another example of fate affecting his life, Miller petitioned his family to employ famed Finnish architect Eliel Saarinen, which they did.

"My father was on the Building Committee and I started yakking at him: 'Why don't you guys pioneer?' said Miller. 'Why don't you take a chance?' And they said, 'What do you mean?' They [went to Michigan and] met Saarinen who then came to Columbus to talk not only to the Building Committee but also to the congregation. He didn't do any designs. In fact, he wouldn't even agree to do the building at all at first." But Miller's father talked him into it.

Completed in 1942, First Christian was the first modern church built in America, and the first example of modern architecture in Columbus. The congregation was captivated by the building with absolute minimum of objection and the community was appalled. "They said: 'Wonder when they're going to move in the machinery?'"[5] Miller would recall.

Critically, this project was the reason Miller met Eliel's son, Eero, who "used to come (to Columbus) as a student… and if the old men were busy we all had lots of time and we used to go out at night for hamburgers… and have endless conversations about everything."[6]

While both were Yale graduates, Miller, though a year younger, was three classes ahead of Eero, and they hadn't gotten to know each other in New Haven. Miller and Eero became extremely close (son Will says Eero was one of his dad's three or four best friends).

Miller went on to commission Eero to do three projects in the 1950s: a summer house on the family compound in the Muskoka region of Ontario (some 150 miles north of Toronto), the Irwin Union Bank's central office, and Miller's year-round Columbus home at 2760 Highland Way, which remains one of the most significant architectural landmarks in the country.

In 1955, Miller once again got the opportunity to express his faith through architecture, alongside his good friend Eero Saarinen. The Millers and over forty other families had decided to leave First Christian Church for theological reasons (among other things, Miller felt that women should have a greater role in church leadership and that the type of baptism one undergoes should be a choice).[7] They had no idea that they wouldn't move into their new church for nearly ten years.

The congregation initially would meet Sundays in members' houses, then at Saint Paul's Episcopal Church, and finally at the Caldwell Mansion they'd bought on Twenty-Fifth Street.[8] This interlude occurred when Miller was between the ages of forty-six and fifty-five—years of peak demands and maximum stress from both his business and pro bono endeavors. As a deeply spiritual individual, Miller had to have desperately desired for himself and his family their own church to regroup spiritually.

He was in a position to do something about the timing. Normally, Miller seemed to want to be nothing but another ordinary member. While deeply spiritual in terms of attending service every Sunday he was in town, treating all persons with respect, regardless of color, gender, or creed, regularly reading the Bible, and giving 35 percent of his pretax income to charity, Miller, according to now deceased John Bean, his pastor for twenty-five years between 1967 and 1992, "never spoke in congregational meetings, never participated in any controversial issues, never sat on any committee [except architecture], and never played his violin at the church."[9] Not wanting to set the pace in annual fund-raising, his pledge (always the largest) was last. He felt, Bean explained, that "the members must have ownership of the congregation because he insisted it was not his church" (and we saw earlier how Miller put up no argument when the congregants opposed his request to be buried in a crypt on church property.)[10]

Miller agreed, however, to chair the all-important architectural committee. Not surprisingly, the committee picked Eero Saarinen to do the church and, as Miller explained,

> The greater part of a year was spent in talk and planning before any design work was started. We covered the following grounds:
>
> 1. The church should be an integrated whole, with the sanctuary and worship dominant… This led to a single structure sheltered by one roof …
>
> 2. The church should express in its physical arrangements the fact that the local congregation is very much a family whose members draw strength from one another. This gradually led to the hexagonal shape of the sanctuary…
>
> 3. The Holy Communion was to be the central part and climax of the worship service. This led to the placing of the large table in the center of the sanctuary …
>
> 4. The Architectural Committee reminded itself that there was no certainty as what type of worship service might be performed in this sanctuary a hundred or two hundred years hence… Therefore, studies were made as to whether all kinds of Christian services could be

performed efficiently in our new sanctuary… we felt a responsibility to future congregations."[11]

At this point, Eero was working on an international stage. In the 1950s, he had designed the CBS Building in New York City, the TWA terminal at Kennedy Airport, and the Gateway Arch in Saint Louis. He was pictured on the cover of *Time* magazine in 1956.

Meanwhile, Miller, who would later become a "successor" trustee of the Yale Corporation, pushed his alma mater to adopt a policy that "only great architects are allowed to submit drawings." With Miller's support certainly not hurting him, Eero was asked to design not only the Ingalls hockey rink (dubbed "the Whale") but Yale's first ever non-Gothic-style dormitories—business brisk enough to cause Eero to move his office from Cranbrook, Michigan, to Hamden, Connecticut.

Eero's busy schedule and surging backlog[12] led to major delays in design and therefore construction. On April 5, 1961, Miller wrote Saarinen to express anguish that "the architect was selected now over two years ago [but] we have no idea when the church will be ready for bids… The reaction of the congregation frightens us… The people of the church haven't got mad… they have simply given up… If this church doesn't come off pretty soon, I think the congregation might fall apart."[13]

Replying on April 18, 1961, Saarinen informed Miller that the church "needs my concentrated time for a week or perhaps two weeks," but because his firm was swamped with other jobs, and Saarinen noted that

> things really don't look open until about the middle or end of September. Irwin, there is nothing I want more than to get your church to move through this office. But before that, a very important step has to happen. We have to finally solve the church so that the church can become a great building… I really, really want to solve it so that as an architect when I face St. Peter am

able to say that of the 20-30-40 buildings I did during
my lifetime, one of the most important and one of
the best in my mind was a church I did in Columbus,
Indiana, because that church has a real idea in the way
worship is expressed by the architecture, and a real spirit
that speaks forth to all Christians as a witness to their
faith.[14]

But Saarinen never did get to finish his church. Time on earth,
unfortunately, had run out for Eero, who, finally pleased with his plans
(his fifth iteration) for North Christian,[15] died that September while
in surgery for a brain tumor. He was just fifty-one years old. Miller
designed and organized Eero's funeral. While his works for Miller were
few in number, Eero and his legacy would continue to have significant
impact on Miller and Columbus.

It was largely Eero's talent that had lifted the sights and spirits of
Miller and his hometown. Two decades later when helping to set up a
chair at Yale in his friend's memory, Miller wrote, "Eero Saarinen will
undoubtedly emerge as the greatest architect of his generation. His
qualities of thoughtful innovation, warm concerns for humans, disdain
of fashions and identification with the needs of his clients are all too
rare nowadays."[16]

Saarinen's unfinished projects, including North Christian Church,
were handed off to Kevin Roche, which would mark the beginning of
another fruitful collaboration between Miller, the visionary, and his
architect. Roche finished the design of North Christian Church, whose
first service was held March 8, 1964.

It was Eero who also introduced Miller to pioneering architect Harry
Weese. "Columbus had a new mayor who asked several of us in local
industries to do something about what would now be called 'affordable
housing' for the area," Miller later recalled. "I, in turn, asked Eero
Saarinen who would be his choice of a young, creative architect. The

result was [we] visited Harry in Chicago. We were charmed by our meeting and commissioned him to do a large number of housing units [which] are still very successful and popular. Harry was also the first architect selected by the local school board to do an elementary school under the Cummins Foundation Plan."[17]

It is interesting to note that, deliberately or by happenstance, Miller commissioned the first of Cummins's modern architectural projects overseas, well ahead of any avant-garde construction domestically. Cummins's first foreign factory, in Shotts, Scotland, was designed by Harry Weese and completed in 1958—it was so unusual that locals referred to it as "the crashed Ford 'Tri-Motor' Airplane."

Weese's first major project for Cummins in Columbus (the technical center) was not completed until ten years later in 1968. Likewise, Kevin Roche created Cummins's Darlington, England, facilities eight years ahead of his first factory for Cummins in the United States, the Walesboro components plant. Perhaps Miller wanted to get his feet wet out of sight.

Weese, in 1963, wrote Miller, "I've reached the plateau that you and Eero plotted for me, in the sense that the work now has the scope and challenge that will stretch me to the limit."[18] Years later, in 1987, Miller wrote Weese, "You are still highly respected in Weeseville [a.k.a. Columbus] and growing. Your work will never be as dated as will that of the post-moderns, and will serve much longer. Don't fall to the temptation to join them."[19]

Collectively, the trio of Eero and his two protégés, Kevin Roche and Harry Weese, completed an astounding nineteen of the thirty-four nonschool architectural projects in Columbus over five decades (1950–1999). The next closest firm, Skidmore, Owings & Merrill, did a grand total of two jobs.[20] Think principally of Eero Saarinen, Kevin Roche, and Harry Weese when considering Columbus's architecture.

Despite the impact that Miller's building projects had on Columbus, he had a tendency to remain relatively anonymous throughout the process. The most notable example certainly was the offer in 1957 to Columbus's school board to fund architectural fees for new schools by the Cummins Engine Foundation (set up in 1954 with 5 percent of the company's pretax profits earmarked for local charitable use). Miller asserted that "the most important single service performed by government in this community is education. Cummins is willing to pay our share."[21]

It was a hugely successful endeavor that involved construction of fourteen new schools in Bartholomew County over the next forty-five years (one in the 1950s, eight in the 1960s, three in the 1970s, two in the 1980s, plus seven "additions" in the 1990s).[22]

Nonschool construction embodying modern design grew apace, with thirty-four buildings erected over the last half of the century—nineteen in the 1960s and 1970s alone. Twenty-three of the thirty-four projects were either Cummins Engine facilities (e.g., the technical center) or other Miller-involved projects (e.g., headquarters of Irwin Union Bank or his home at 2760 Highland Way). Miller also had an indirect yet understandable influence in other local work. Don Tull, Cummins's president, sat on the board of First Baptist Church (built in 1963), and Jim Henderson, a Cummins vice president at the time, was a director of Indiana Bell Telephone, whose switching center was constructed in 1978.

Another example of Miller being involved yet invisible with architecture was a new post office for Columbus. Learning in 1965 that Uncle Sam planned to replace its old facility, Miller directed Dick Stoner, Cummins's executive vice president, to meet in Washington with then first-term Congressman Lee Hamilton and Postmaster General Larry O'Brien, and, per Hamilton, Lyndon B. Johnson, president of the United States (who appointed Miller to chair four separate, special commissions during his five years in office) wandered in and told O'Brien, "You give this Congressman anything he wants."[23]

Miller later noted, "The Post Office Department specified the floor plan in detail and allowed the architect only to put a skin on the structure. This whole experience was an unhappy one. The Department very strongly did not want an outside architect and the relationship in which I was not involved between architect and client was difficult throughout."[24] Notably, the new post office represented the first use in Columbus of COR-TEN steel (that deliberately rusts) and had earlier been employed by Roche in the design of the East Moline, Illinois, headquarters of Deere & Co., whose chairman, William Hewitt, was a good friend of Miller. (It is noteworthy that Roche had already employed COR-TEN on the plants in Darlington, England.)[25]

Miller disavowed possessing an agenda to redo his hometown according to modern tastes. In fact, he would later agree with an interviewer on the *Today Show* that "there's no plan to the town at all." "Personally," Miller explained, "I feel that process is more important that progress, and that the democratic process with a certain amount of mess in it is the way Americans like to live. This is a pluralistic society, with a lot of individuals, and its richness comes out of its variety."[26]

Perhaps Miller best put his thoughts on Columbus's architecture in a letter he wrote in 1976:

> Columbus will always have its lousy areas… but… it is as near a real community as any place I know. People differ furiously among themselves. But I can't think of anyone who is not on speaking terms with his neighbor. There is still racial prejudice, but there is not a part of town in which blacks cannot and do not live.

> The churches have a fund to bail out any stranger who gets thrown into the local slammer, provided he hasn't committed murder … We are organized to guarantee a vigorous legal aid program and have a Human Rights Commission.

> All these we are as proud of as the architecture and without these evidences of genuine concern the architecture wouldn't be all that much.[27]

Miller, always unobtrusive, took great satisfaction from architectural enhancements to his community. He observed to a close friend that Mount Healthy Elementary School in a rural setting "is probably the best of the schools we have built."[28]

Perhaps no piece of architecture in Columbus pleased Miller as much as the family's gift of the Large Arch, a bronze sculpture by Henry Moore, about which he wrote so beautifully in 1971 to the editorial director of *Time* magazine: "We have just finished a remarkable new plaza here. It is surrounded by a 30-year old church designed by Eliel Saarinen, and a brand new county library by I. M. Pei. In its center is one of the largest sculptures which Henry Moore has ever done, commissioned for the spot. This is now one of the great [public] spaces in America."[29]

Extending an invitation to Moore himself to attend the dedication, Miller expressed himself so lyrically:

> The Arch is now in place, and we have had nearly a full week to become acquainted with it:
>
> It is an addition to our community and our personal lives that is really beyond description. It is not my habit to speak extravagantly, so that you must know that I write out of a very deep response to this noble work. There are two local schools nearby. As the Arch was being unloaded and set in place, classes were dismissed and several hundred children, from ages 6 to 16, watched the whole operation.
>
> The community comes to see it, touch it, walk around and through it, sketch it until late hours at night, and, in a most real and human way it has now become a physical and spiritual center of our town. It has made the plaza of which it is the focus one of the finest spaces in America.[30]

With characteristic anonymity and humility, Miller would not allow placement of a plaque informing visitors of his family's donation.[31]

Miller called the area bounded by the Irwin mansion, Eeliel Saarinen's First Christian Church, Henry Moore's Large Arch, and I.M. Pei's county library "one of the great public spaces in America."

Provided by Rhonda Bolner, Columbus, Indiana

8

The Search for Purpose

After the death of his father in 1947 and the retirement of Clessie in 1951, Miller took on increased duties. Yet he managed his responsibilities with an oddly distant touch and he had yet to forge any real paths on his own. While his family still controlled four businesses (Cummins Engine Company [by far the largest], Irwin Union Bank, Purity Stores, and Union Starch and Refining), Miller didn't actually "run" any of them—Robert Huthsteiner ran Cummins, Ed Lauther managed the bank, John Niven headed up Purity Stores, and George Newlin was at Starch. He also had reporting to him one or more full-time assistants— usually someone fresh out of graduate business school—that often went on to join one of the companies. If Miller ended up with a particularly big project—like producing the final report on Lyndon B. Johnson's study on trade with the Soviet Union in 1965—he would simply borrow an executive for the assignment (in this case, James A. Henderson).

Crucially, Miller had set up his office on the second floor of 301 Washington Street, a move that physically separated him from his businesses and hugely helped him manage his time. He maintained this practice for the rest of his life.

Yet Miller's manner in organizing himself like this in no way signaled that he was lazy. "He had incredible energy," Ed Booth recalls.[1] Rather, "he never saw leadership as a solo effort. It was always a shared, team effort," his son Will maintains.[2] But Will also notes that around this time, his father was stricken with polio. In the summer of 1949, he indeed wrote to Clessie that he had "a light attack of polio," but it was almost as an aside, buried in a business update.[3] His son Will, however, maintains that "it nearly killed him!"[4] For certain, polio ended his dad's tennis playing and resulted in a permanent, slight limp in his gait. It well might have honed his penchant to delegate and not to hog the limelight. (Maybe, too, a near-constant reminder of his mortality.)

And there was most certainly a fire burning inside of him to make an impact—in business, in his community, and beyond.

He freed up time by no longer visiting customers,[5] touring Cummins's Columbus facilities,[6] or traveling other than once to China, a huge emerging market for the company.[7] In short, he cut himself a lot of slack. Fred Reams, the highly successful manager of Cummins's pension portfolio, recalls, "He juggled his time very well."[8] And B. Joseph White, VP of personnel in the 1980s, remarks, "I never had a sense he spread himself too thin."[9] It allowed Miller to leverage his time not just over the family's businesses but also over the sundry pro bono causes in which he had gotten or soon would be involved.

In the fifties, Miller's focus was local. Joining their three daughters, two boys were born to the Millers in the 1950s—Hugh in 1951 and Will in 1956—all of whom attended Columbus's public schools through eighth grade and then went east to boarding school, like their dad and Aunt Clementine. But Miller had also always considered the Cummins community family, and he became more outspoken than ever about workers' rights. This would become one of the most important moments in Miller's legacy.

Workers' rights were, in fact, the only rights cause in which Miller was deeply engaged throughout this decade, as civil rights wasn't yet on his or most people's radars yet—in 1960, the nonwhite population of Columbus was 278, and its schools had no "Negro teachers" in 1961. His son Will explains that his dad was more comfortable with people off the shop floor than customers or upper management. He assumed the hourly (say, compared with his foreman) was right.[10]

Miller was quoted in 1949 by the *Indianapolis News*, saying: "It's the fashion these days to run down the working man but our employees are conscientious, able, and doing a good job. If we have labor trouble, we'll have to look to management because it would be our fault."[11] A dozen years later, he told a reporter that "he wouldn't want to run a plant without a strong responsible union [which] holds a mirror up to management, showing us things that we otherwise couldn't see."[12]

Miller's crusade for the common man extended into his hometown, Columbus. Miller was active in the 1950s in Columbus's chamber of commerce, serving as president for a number of years. [13] His main focus, though, was on "brick and mortar": "Columbus needs to provide homes, churches, schools, recreational and cultural facilities that will make our town a place where people will prefer to live."[14] These were causes that dovetailed nicely with his passion for architecture.

Miller had the time to write and deliver beautifully crafted Sunday school lessons for his congregation at First Christian Church.[15] Later, after cutting ties with First Christian, he helped build North Christian Church.[16] According to the Christian Theological Society, "the congregants [future NCC] began meeting in October 1955 in members' homes on Sunday evenings and then at Saint Paul's Episcopal Church."[17] In the meantime, the congregants had contracted Saarinen to design their new church.

Cummins Engine, meanwhile, was chugging along rather smoothly. It was starting to reap the benefits of construction of the US interstate highway system under President Dwight D. Eisenhower, who had seen firsthand how the autobahn had benefited Nazi Germany. Cummins's sales would grow 2.2 times in the 1950s.

The arithmetic was simple. Trucks were taking freight from railroads, diesels were replacing gasoline engines in these trucks, and Cummins was taking share from other diesel engine builders. Physically, Cummins Engine would surge from a single factory in 1956 (venerable Plant #1 in Columbus) to eleven plants (six overseas) in 1965. The company went public in 1958. Miller and his family owned 65 percent of Cummins's stock in 1959.[18]

Facilitating this growth, Cummins's replacement of an old DC-3 airplane with a new Convair turboprop in 1957 made it possible for Miller to get to and from the East Coast the same day, for the first time.[19]

Serving on boards where he could let his passions drive change occupied most of his time. Aside from a couple of corporate boards in New York City (Chemical Bank and Trust and Equitable Life), Miller, for now, kept things local: Indiana National Bank, Butler University, and Christian Theological Seminary, of which he became Chairman in 1958. Yet his board duties were set to expand exponentially.

In the summer of 1954, the Millers attended a luncheon in Bloomington, Indiana, at the home of their longtime friend and president of Indiana University, Herman Wells, where Miller was introduced to Whitney Griswold, president of Yale University.

Evidently intrigued with the soft-spoken Hoosier, Griswold appointed Miller to the University Council in 1956 and Miller quickly became chairman of the council's Committee on Religious Life and Study, with bigger assignments to come. Miller would refer to the council "as a sort of farm club for the Corporation."[20]

"The Corporation" is what Yale calls its board of directors, which, aside from the president, consists of two groups—ten successor trustees appointed to serve to age sixty-seven and six alumni fellows, one elected each year, who serve six years. In 1959, after losing an election as an alumni fellow, Miller was appointed a successor trustee to serve until 1977 (when he turned sixty-eight).

It seems largely due to the overlap of several Yale trustees on the Ford Foundation, Miller was asked to become a trustee there too in 1961. Serving on the boards of Yale and the Ford Foundation would entail a great deal of Miller's time. Yale trustees met nine times per year and held two-day meetings each time and then a further four times on a development board (for a total of twenty-two days). Ford Foundation board members had four two-day meetings per year, for a total of eight days. Combined, they would take up thirty days of Miller's time per year at a minimum, because there would be ad hoc sessions scheduled from time to time in New York City.

Henry ("Sam") Chauncey Jr., who, as chief of staff, had a ringside seat at Yale University during the turbulent decades of the 1960s and 1970s, states, "Miller was the best trustee of the twentieth century among some very fine ones. He was devoted to Yale for all the right reasons. More trustees wanted to keep Yale the way it used to be—when they were undergraduates. Miller felt 'we must always be moving forward.'"[21] For Miller, this largely meant the increased enrollment of women and African Americans.

Miller's first major contribution to his alma mater concerned architecture. According to Chauncey, Miller was appalled at the first building erected on Griswold's watch in the mid-1950s, a physics lab, and convinced Griswold that innovative architecture (not "continuous Gothic") was important to the intellectual life of a community (reminiscent of the architectural scheme for new-school construction then occurring in Columbus, Indiana). Miller got Griswold to hire Eero Saarinen to create a master plan for Yale.[22] It helped, of course, that Eero was a Yale alum of the early 1930s (like Miller and Griswold) and that he'd just been featured on the cover of *Time* magazine.

In short order, Eero received so many assignments from Yale that he moved his office from Michigan to suburban New Haven (a backlog, ironically, that would significantly slip the construction schedule of Miller's North Christian Church in Indiana).

In 1958, Miller ran for a six-year term as alumni fellow of the corporation but lost (presumably due to his liberal reputation). In 1959, however, Miller was appointed by the corporation a successor trustee (which would last for eighteen years). These ten trustees (successors to the ten Protestant ministers that had founded Yale in the 1700s) were an awesome lot. As example, they included William McChesney Martin, head of the Federal Reserve Bank; Juan T. Trippe, founder and chairman of Pan American Airways; J. Richardson Dilworth, financial manager of the Rockefeller Foundation; William Bundy, national security advisor at the Defense Department; and John Hay ("Jock") Whitney, owner of the *New York Herald Tribune*.[23]

In the late 1950s and early 1960s, Miller assumed an absolutely astonishing amount of incremental pro bono work: 1958, chairman of the board, Christian Theological Seminary (that he'd just pried loose from Butler University); 1959, successor trustee, the Yale Corporation, and also director, American Telephone & Telegraph; and 1961, trustee, Ford Foundation.

On top of this increased activity, he agreed to chair the architectural committee in charge of constructing North Christian Church, though he stipulated it only meet nights when he was in town and always complete its agenda each time.[24] He boosted the number of speeches from one per year in the 1950s to three per year in the 1960s, or the equivalent of two extra weeks' work per year,[25] and he oversaw construction of Otter Creek Golf Course, which Cummins gave to Columbus and he dedicated in 1964 with his wonderfully eloquent speech—which some people call his "Gettysburg Address" (both were brief—Miller's 188 words versus Lincoln's 272).

"*W*hy should an industrial company, organized for profit, think it a good and right thing to take a million dollars and more, of that profit, and give it to this community in the form of this golf course and club house? Why, instead, isn't Cummins—the largest taxpayer in the county, spending the same energy to try to get its taxes reduced, the cost of education cut, the cost of city government cut, less money spent on streets and utilities and schools?

"This answer is that we would like to see this community come to be not the cheapest community in America, but the very best community of its size in the country. We would like to see it become the city in which the smartest, the ablest, the best young families anywhere would like to live . . . a community that is open in every single respect to persons of every race, color and opinion, that makes them feel welcome and at home here . . . a community which will offer their children the best education available anywhere . . . a community of strong, outspoken churches, of genuine cultural interests, exciting opportunities for recreation . . . a community whose citizens are themselves well-paid and who will not tolerate poverty for others, or slums in their midst.

"No such community can be built without citizens determined to make their community best, without city government which works boldly— ahead of its problems, and not always struggling to catch up—and without money sufficient to get the job done.

"So Cummins is not for cheap education, or inadequate, poorly-paid government, or second-rate facilities or low taxes just for the sake of low taxes. Our concern is to help get the most for our dollar, to help build this community into the best in the nation. And we are happy to pay our share, whether in work, or in taxes, or in gifts like this one."

Some called Miller's 1964 speech, dedicating Otter Creek Golf Course as a gift from Cummins Engine to the community, his "Gettysburg address". Provided by the Indiana Historical Society

He undertook these pro bono commitments evidently because he fervently believed in these causes. Also, it allowed him to connect with movers and shakers in business, labor, religion, government, academia, and the arts. And he got to travel to interesting places, such as Russia with the National Council of Churches and Africa with the Ford Foundation. Then Miller could do as he pleased with Cummins—he and his family owned 65 percent of its shares in 1959,[26] and although the company had gone public in 1958, it had only one "outsider" on its board of directors as the decade of the 1960s began: Seymour Dribben, his roommate at Taft and Oxford, now an officer at Chemical Bank in New York City.[27]

His schedule, while manageable in the early fifties, became backbreaking by decade's end. As an example, his personal planner for June 1962 shows that he was to speak at commencements at three universities (Marian, Oberlin, and Princeton), attend a three-day meeting in New York City at the National Council of Churches, as well as six other board meetings: Indiana National Bank, Indianapolis, AT&T, and Ford Foundation (two days) in New York, and Irwin Union Bank, Cummins, and Union Starch in Columbus — all in a single month![28]

His full-year 1965 calendar, as typed by his secretary, involved fifty trips just to New York and New Haven (and he was likely to be attending two or three meetings on some of these trips). It meant one round trip per week to the East Coast.[29]

No cause was as dear to Miller as his work with the National Council of Churches. As shown in the table below, NCC fills up more boxes at the Irwin-SweeneyMiller collection at the Indiana Historical Society than anything except Cummins Engine and is nearly three times the volume of the third and fourth categories, Yale University and the Ford Foundation.

It is worth noting that, based on the amount of material archived, NCC took up by far the greatest portion of Miller's pro bono efforts in the 1960s (where as Yale University and the Ford Foundation assumed their highest portion of his time in the 1970s). He gave eleven speeches between 1960 and 1963, usually devoted to civil rights.[30] On behalf of NCC, he led a three-week trip of twelve American churchmen to the Soviet Union to learn the status of their religiosity. Not only was there a reciprocal trip to the United States by Soviet religious people, but Miller would later conduct similar visits to India and Africa.[31]

Distribution of Miller's Major Pro-Bono Efforts by Decade Based on Number of Folders in ISM Collection:

	1950s	1960s	1970s	1980s	1990s	Total
NCC[#]	50%	42%	8%			100%
Yale University[*]	19%	62%	13%	6%		100%
Ford Foundation[**]	2%	64%	33%	11%		100%

[#]   JIM was lay chairman from 1960 to 1963
[*]   JIM served as successor trustee from 1959 to 1977
[**]   JIM served as trustee from 1961 to 1979

After serving the National Council of Churches in various spot assignments in the 1950s, Miller became its first lay chairman (a part-time assignment) in November 1960, the month Kennedy was elected, and he served until November 1963, the month Kennedy was assassinated. Miller described NCC as "a voluntary association of 34 Protestant and Orthodox communions in the United States with a membership of more than 40 million people."[32]

Likely what caused Miller's assignment was the fact that, two years earlier (in 1958), he had pried loose from Butler University Christian Theological Seminary, the Disciples' largest ministerial school, of which he was then Chairman.[33] Probably, too, the leaders of NCC saw in Miller a deeply convinced ecumenicist. Speaking at the International Convention of Christian Churches (Disciples of Christ) in 1961, Miller declared:

"I am bound to this brotherhood of ours by ties that are stronger than I had ever guessed in my youth. I am bound to it by conviction. Its freedom, its confession, its warm generous inclusive love are a part of my life. I am bound to it by sentiment. I have grown up among Disciples, stuffed myself to the point of pain at church dinners with Disciples. I have dressed up for church pageants, taught Sunday school classes, and sung in choirs with Disciples. I am bound to it by history. Both of my grandfathers were Disciples ministers. I am bound to this brotherhood in every possible way, and I cherish these ties." [34]

In 1962, Miller wrote, "The most serious weakness of Christianity in the world is its split and divided witness. This can be corrected only when various branches of Christendom are able to find ways of witnessing together. By bringing together representatives from 34 Protestant and Orthodox groups... The National Council points to the fact that Protestants in all denominations are united in their loyalty to Christ."[35] As a Christian church elder wrote years later, Miller's life consisted both of "proclamation" and "social involvement" (i.e., he not only "spoke out" but "did good deeds").[36]

Miller would explain that the NCC "distributes food, drugs and clothing to the needy, conducts Christian education, speaks to Christians everywhere about important situations... but unlike the Roman Catholic Church does not and cannot pronounce official positions that are binding on Christians."[37]

9

A Leader Emerges

It didn't take long for Miller's outside obligations to have an effect on his role at Cummins. But it was also one of the most productive and pivotal times in his life.

Ironically, Miller accepted his two major pro bono undertakings—the National Council of Churches and Yale University—with little appreciation of the commitment involved (mental, physical, and temporal!). Plus, racial tensions in the United States in the late 1950s were quiescent, relative to the next decade, when they would become the major focus for the NCC, Yale, and, indeed, America as a whole. Miller once recalled, "Civil rights wasn't even in [President John F.] Kennedy's state of the union address in January 1961, so this came with a rush on the country... There really was no concern about race [with the NCC]... throughout the fifties, the church was asleep on the subject of race."[1]

Miller "ascended to the Presidency of the [NCC] just as the first sit-ins were rumbling across the south" when civil rights unrest exploded in the United States. "He soon helped form the Council's Commission on Religion and Race, whose energetic support of civil rights earned it an unremitting attack from right-wing extremists as 'soft on communism'... He helped to organize the 'March on Washington,' helped the President on civil rights bills, and was one of the Church leaders to organize the National Conference on Race and Religion in 1963."[2] (Kennedy, who did not succeed in getting civil rights legislation passed by Congress, would not attend, although it would be held on the hundredth anniversary of Lincoln's Gettysburg Address.)

Martin Luther King called Miller the most socially responsible businessman in the country.[3]

Miller paid a price for his opposition to racial discrimination, which he described as "a sort of national insanity."[4] After a speech in a Presbyterian Church in Pasadena, California, in October 1961, "The opposition... for nearly three hours... fired a barrage of questions" (e.g., "Is it not true that the National Council is soft on Communism?") Miller, though, "held his own throughout" and "answered questions until after 11:00 p.m. Not once did he lose control of the situation or display anger," saying, "If I thought [the Council] was infiltrated [by Communists], I wouldn't lend my name or time or influence to it."[5]

Caterpillar, Cummins Engine's rival, even ran advertisements in southern states that said "Buy from CAT, not Cummins—their CEO is fighting for N——!," Will Miller recalls his father telling him.[6]

The president of the American Farm Bureau, who knew Miller (addressing him as Irwin), on September 27, 1963, in regard to the march on Washington, wrote to ask if it were true that the NCC "had purchased 80,000 lunches to distribute in Washington on August 26 and that the cost for this food together with 75,000 'Freedom' song books was paid for out of Church World Service funds."

Miller replied that the NCC did contribute to the cost of food and song sheets. "Nearly every... denomination has now publicly committed itself in words and dollars to support... racial justice and had emphasized the Christian responsibility of white Christians to share the burden of their negro brothers, and not leave the struggle to them alone."[7]

Change was afoot at Yale, too, and Miller would lead the university into the next decade. Just like all of the other successor trustees of the Yale Corporation, Miller was a WASP (white Anglo-Saxon protestant), came from a rich family, attended boarding school and an ivy-league college, and had served as a junior officer in the war. But he couldn't have been more different. By then, he was already a veteran of fighting bigotry of any type—in the US Navy, his company, his hometown, and, now as lay chairman of the National Council of Churches, where he would work to "organize the 1963 'March on Washington' helping legitimize Martin Luther King and his movement."[8] Antibigotry was hardwired in his DNA and suffused in his religiosity.

As "black students began non-violent sit-ins at segregated Woolworth's lunch counters in the South,"[9] Yale University, like its peers, seemed unfazed—just three black males matriculated at New Haven in 1960.[10] These early days, the one member of the administration to display real zeal for civil rights was Yale's Chaplain, William Sloane Coffin, who took part in numerous protests, including at great personal risk helping blacks register to vote in the South.[11]

Yale president Whitney Griswold died of cancer in April 1963, making way for Kingman Brewster. Ten years Miller's junior, Brewster had been provost for just three years and earlier had been a professor at Harvard Law School—not much preparation for the trials that lay ahead. But "Kingman had learned from Whitney Griswold how valuable was Miller, and Miller was his favorite trustee, though Brewster wouldn't admit this," said Sam Chauncey, and related that Miller was by far the most informed trustee about detailed goings-on at the university. In addition to attending every meeting of the Corporation, Miller stayed in very close touch with Brewster via letters—often using a felt color pen displaying his mood—and late-night phone calls.[12] "Miller motivated colleagues and institutions to seek progressive changes," Chauncey says. "He put backbone into men like Brewster, pushed them to modernize their organizations, and spurred them on to make the controversial decisions that they knew were the correct ones."[13]

When in June 1964 Yale "became one of the first [universities] to award an honorary degree to the Reverend Martin Luther King, Jr.," Miller wrote one of many alumni who were vigorously opposed to the leftist lurch of their alma mater:

> We combat best [the threat of worldwide Communism] by making our country so strong and healthy... that the Communist virus finds no fertile soil among us.

This means, among other things, the elimination of persistent poverty, the reduction of unemployment... and the extension of equal freedom, dignity and opportunity to every segment of our people. We have no sickness in our nation more apt to turn mortal than that which denies the full fruits of a free society to those of Negro ancestry. Reverend King represents in my opinion the most responsible and Christian effort of Negroes to gain what they should never have been denied.[14]

As the decade of the 1960s progressed, tension between reactionary alumni and a progressive administration grew. This is one example:

In the spring of 1966, Admissions Director R. Inslee ("Inky") Cark was summoned before the Yale Corporation to report directly on the changes in policy he had implemented since his appointment by [Kingman] Brewster the year before.

One of the Corporation members[15] said [in regards to the Class of 1970]: "You're admitting an entirely different class than we're used to. You're admitting them for a different purpose than training leaders..." Clark responded that, in a changing America, leaders might come from non-traditional sources, including public high school graduates, Jews, minorities, and even women. His interlocutor shot back, "You're talking about Jews and public school graduates as leaders. Look around you at this table"—he waved a hand at Brewster, [John V.] Lindsay, Moore, Bill Bundy and the other distinguished men assembled there. 'These are America's leaders. There are no Jews here. There are no public school graduates here.

No aspect of Kingman Brewster's presidency stirred more debate than the overhaul of Yale's undergraduate admissions... in the second half of the 1960s, Brewster, Bundy... and the rest devoted themselves to the cause of equality of opportunity.[16]

Yale continued to enroll more black kids—forty-three entered in 1968,[17] and went fully coed in the fall of 1969, admitting five hundred women across three classes (yet maintaining the same number of men).[18]

In a fitting coda to cap the ending of the most tumultuous decade in the school's long history, Miller told a convocation on November 14, 1968, in New Haven, "Yale is not the Yale that you and I knew... and thank God for that—instead it is embarked on a responsible, creative evolution in service to the nation in the midst of one of the nation's most critical periods."[19]

While the National Council of Churches and the Yale Corporation were Miller's most beloved causes, the Ford Foundation would seem the closest runner-up. The years of service at Ford—1961–1979—closely overlapped those serving Yale. By the 1960s, the Ford Foundation was "by far the largest of America's seventeen thousand foundations—its $3 billion endowment was three and a half times the size of its nearest competitor, the Rockefeller Foundation."[20] The Ford Foundation was, then, mostly focused on improving salaries of the faculties of America's colleges and universities: "Of the $1.5 billion in grants [it] made between 1950 and 1965, about $1 billion had gone to educational affairs."[21]

But, as discussed earlier, civil rights had become the country's number-one issue in the early 1960s, and Miller was recruited to become a Ford trustee by John McCloy, renowned diplomat and himself a trustee, because "I was also president of the National Council of Churches [which] was entering its field of intense preoccupation with race and social programs."[22]

When the Ford Foundation's president retired in 1965, Miller was in the thick of recruiting a replacement. "We went over a very long list of people… One quality above anything else… the head of the Foundation ought to be a person who had demonstrated that he really had a first-class mind, with a broad range of interests [and]… be a perpetual learner… and McGeorge Bundy's name clearly came out first."[23]

Yale alumnus and probably as close a friend as Miller to its president, Kingman Brewster, Bundy was head of the National Security Council, under President Lyndon Johnson, but he had become bitterly opposed to America's involvement in the Vietnam War and had decided to quit the administration. "Irwin Miller had worked with Bundy at the White House as Chairman of a Presidential Commission on Trade with the Soviet Bloc, and [Miller said] 'I had heard a lot about Mac from Kingman Brewster.'"[24]

Remarkably, "McGeorge Bundy had not had significant contact with the underprivileged by the time he left the White House for the Ford Foundation at the end of February, 1966."[25] "By his own admission, Bundy had spent little time thinking about black-white relations before he went to Ford… 'Race was a whole new ball game for Mac and Kingman', said Harold ('Doc') Howe—a Yale classmate of Bundy [who had offered a 'tap' to Skull and Bones that Brewster refused]."[26] "Bundy educated himself by setting aside the first half of each workday morning for reading, and by meeting with black leaders… speaking on behalf of his Foundation, Bundy declared that 'full equality of all American Negroes is now the most urgent concern in this country' and would henceforth be the most important priority of the Ford Foundation as well."[27]

We strongly believe that Miller directly caused and forcibly backed Bundy's sudden transformation of the Ford Foundation's top priority from college teachers' salaries to black people's civil rights. No white American had Miller's passion for "helping the underdog," and we can visualize Miller working the trustees to approve the sea change in its direction.

That Miller took this assignment with utmost sincerity and dedication is seen in a letter a fellow trustee and eminent lawyer, Judge Charles E. Wyzanski Jr. of the US District Court in Boston wrote him: "When we served together on the Ford Foundation Board… you were the best of trustees—the soundest in judgment, the wisest in knowledge, and the most far-seeing in regard to fundamental values."[28]

As another sign of his groundedness in civil rights, Miller (likely through his friend John V. Lindsay) had gotten to know Franklin A. Thomas, the African American CEO of Bedford Stuyvesant Restoration Corp., whose aim was rebuilding a Brooklyn ghetto and whose funding came from the Ford Foundation, among other sources. Thomas would join the board of directors of Cummins in 1973 (serving until 2003). And, learning on a foundation trip to India in 1979, that Bundy planned to resign as president, Miller and Donald S. Perkins (fellow member of both Ford and Cummins boards) decided at the Calcutta airport to propose that Thomas succeed Bundy, Perkins recalls.[29] And Thomas would head the Ford Foundation until 1996, meaning, of course, that "Miller's men"—Bundy and Thomas—would lead the Ford Foundation for a combined thirty years!

Miller's efforts on behalf of the Ford Foundation weren't all give; there was some take. In a 1991 interview, Miller stated, "I have found that service outside the business is actually refreshing rather than exhausting. You come back from a good trustees' meeting all fired up with new ideas for your business… I would say the service on the Ford Foundation [relative to time as fellow of the Yale Corporation] gave me more of a window on the world, because it took me to developing countries, into every continent, gave me a chance to visit some of the worst human situations that exist. And that changed forever your attitude… about your own government's policies and about your business activities."[30]

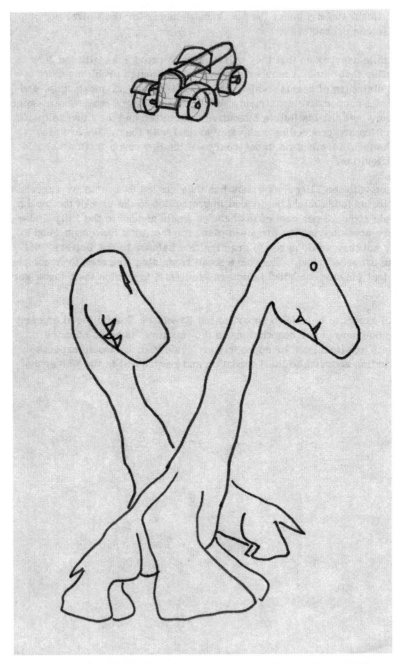

Felt-pen clenched in left fist, Miller was a life-long "doodler",
sketching these images at a Ford Foundation meeting in the 1970s.
Provided by the Indiana Historical Society

Among all the boxes in the ISM collection, there is not one file marked "Irwin Management Company." This is astonishing considering the success of this little-known side venture that surely occupied even more of Miller's precious attention. When time came to ship ISM papers from Columbus to Indianapolis, these particular records were left behind in the basement of 301 Washington Street because IMC (by that point a family foundation spending its last dollars) was still in existence and were subsequently shredded for security purposes, according to longtime employee Sarla Kalsi.[31] A salient part of Miller's life, the story needs telling.

Miller tapped George Newlin from Union Starch and Refining in the mid-1950s to set up and run Irwin Management Company as a vehicle to handle the family's nonCummins investments, essentially securities (stocks and bonds) and real estate. Employing Harold Higgins as its recruiter, Irwin Management grew rapidly. In fact, astonishingly, by the late-1960s, it employed over eighty professionals in its portfolio management group and another dozen or so in its real estate division.[32]

Higgins aimed to get the best people possible. He recruited each year the top students at the top graduate business schools (e.g., Harvard and Stanford). Most were hired as long-term employees for Irwin Management, while some (explicitly or implicitly) were regarded as transients heading after some "seasoning" for positions in the bank or the engine company. In fact, the top three executives under Miller after the 1960s at Cummins started out at Irwin Management: Henry B. Schacht, James A. Henderson, and John T. Hackett.

The top leadership at Irwin Management, particularly on the securities side, was awesome. Garnett Keith, the leader of the portfolio management group, would later serve as chief investment officer (1984–1998) at the Prudential Insurance Company of America; Laurence R. ("Laurie") Hoagland Jr., who ran the portfolio, per se, went on to manage the endowment at Stanford University in the 1990s and recently retired as chief of investing for the Hewlett Foundation; and Fred Reams, a portfolio manager, who later would work at Cummins managing its pension funds that would grow from $185 million to $850 million in the 1980s.[33]

Not wanting Reams to slip through his hands, John T. Hackett, then vice president of finance, in 1981 let Reams "go private" and manage Cummins's pension fund in Reams's own business. Initially, the portfolio management group produced awesome results. "In every sense, it was a hedge fund," recalls Reams. It went long or short, bought bonds or stocks, and employed margin (often using Miller's Cummins shares as collateral). In the early years, the group's performance was astounding. Keith recalls the value of their portfolio doubled in a single year (1968). On the basis of this record, Newlin and Keith wanted to move their offices to Chicago and take on outside clients.

Miller, though, wouldn't agree with them. "Yes, your record's good," Keith recalls him saying, "but I won't let you bring in new investors. I know the risk you'll take, and I don't want to be on the line."[34] Miller's caution was justified. As Reams succinctly remembers: "The s— hit the fan in 1974." The US embargo of Middle East crude caused the price of oil to soar and Cummins shares to plummet from around forty dollars to near ten dollars. Irwin Management, which had been using Miller's shares of Cummins stock to collateralize loans to buy securities, now had to sell these shares (the real-estate holdings obviously were too illiquid to sell quickly). Additionally, Miller wanted money for bequests he had made (to Yale University or Christian Theological Seminary, for example). As a consequence, Irwin Management quickly shrunk its portfolio management team and ultimately terminated that operation by the end of 1975.

Keith contends, "By a factor of ten, Miller had more passion for the engine business than the bank or the investment management business… Cummins Engine was his baby… it had had only sixty-five employees when he joined."

Suggesting that a better option for Miller at the time might have been to sell Cummins and build his fortune with Irwin Management, Keith argues that the leaders of Irwin Management's securities team "went on to great success, while Cummins didn't do anything for a long time. [He] frittered away one of our country's greatest investment operations."[35]

In retrospect, Miller was likely correct to put the future of the engine company ahead of the investment firm—he still felt Cummins had great potential and didn't want to put its employees at risk.

10

Crunch Time for the Engine Company

Miller's extracurricular activities reached their frenzied peak in 1963. It was his third and last and (though, part time) most exhausting year as lay president of the National Council of Churches. And that spring's march on Washington, which he helped organize, directly would assist Lyndon B. Johnson ram civil rights legislation through Congress as president in 1964.

What made Miller believe he could handle this incremental activity? First, he himself still really wasn't running anything—he'd put trusted folks in charge. For example, at Cummins, his flagship enterprise, his number-one and number-two executives were E. Donald Tull and Richard B. Stoner[1]—men for whom he had deep respect and affection. He also had a cadre of intelligent, hardworking people to do staff work, like George W. Newlin. And the engine company had just upgraded its aircraft, which made single-day roundtrips to the east coast possible.[2]

But Miller also had enormous confidence in the earnings potential of the engine company. Cummins had just introduced a family of engines of a V design (the banks for cylinders—three per side on a six-cylinder and four per side on an eight-cylinder—are ninety degrees apart) that were oversquare (the bore, or width of the piston, is greater than the stroke, or length of the piston.) The new oversquare V family consisted of two small engines called VAL (six-cylinder) and VALE (eight-cylinder) and two large engines called VIM (six-cylinder) and

VINE (eight-cylinder). In comparison with the NH, these smaller engines were aimed at the stop-and-go market, where engines were still overwhelmingly gasoline.

Miller's ebullient view was grounded in one of the most amazing documents contained in the ISM collection at the Indiana Historical Society: a handwritten speech he gave at a Cummins management dinner in December of 1961,where he announced that his company's goal is to "become the outstanding investment to be found in security markets in the 1960s" predicated on a "15% annually-compounded growth in sales and profits" (i.e., Cummins stock would be the best performer in the decade of the 1960s).

Acknowledging that a substantial shift from gasoline to diesel engines had already occurred, Miller said these goals would require "having [a] product edge in [a] large variety of sizeable new markets… products of superior excellence and superior earning power. This means VAL, VALE, VIM, VINE, including turbo versions [and] five years from now, complete new line and again in 1970… The limit is not money—this business can generate ample cash to finance growth. It is not lack of opportunity… [The] only thing will stop us [is] people… I believe you fellows are capable of such a record, and I believe if you were in my place, you wouldn't settle for less."[3]

The goal, he said, was "15% annually compounding growth in sales and profits." Since the base year (1960) sales were $136 million, they'd have to climb to $540 million by 1970, and since 1960 profits were $6 million, they'd need to grow to $30 million.

The truth was that Cummins Engine Company needed Miller's attention.

Miller threw his weight behind the oversquare and V engines because he believed Cummins needed to diversify by developing smaller, stop-and-go motors domestically as well as internationally. Of course, Miller was not an engineer. "His technical understanding was not very deep," says a retired engineer in a position to judge, who wishes to remain nameless. Miller's liberal arts background showed through in a letter he wrote Nev Reiners, chief engineer, as its oversquares were released for production: "This company has never given proper attention to the weight of its product. Every time I ask what an engine weighs, no one in the research lab can tell me right away."[4] Words of a dilettante?

One might think Miller would have asked Clessie about oversquares before their aggressive launch, but there is no evidence in the ISM papers that this happened. Years later, Phil Jones, lead designer of the B engine, who came to Columbus in the 1960s from Perkins Engine, said, "When I heard there was a Cummins oversquare engine, I laughed all the way home. An in-line six is the perfect engine. It's simpler and less costly. Everything is balanced."[5]

Signaling a woeful lack of what we today call governance, there was no one then on Cummins's board of directors to challenge Miller's decisions. The lone outside member was, as seen, his high-school and Oxford roommate, Seymour Dribben, a midlevel banker from New York. His two top executives, Don Tull and Dick Stoner, either didn't feel they had sufficient knowledge or didn't feel it was their place to challenge the boss.

The larger version of oversquare motors, the VIMs and the VINEs, "hit the market in volume in 1962 [and] were generating major warranty costs by 1963… [whereas] the average warranty cost on an NH engine in May 1963 was $61 on the VINE the equivalent figure was $1,285"!

"Irwin Miller was aghast… VIM/VINE warranty costs [were] a projected two-year total of $6.5 million [or] more than the total dividends paid these two years."[6]

Unable to make its stop-and-go engines work, but undaunted, Cummins's management decided to make the Vs in Europe and sell them to vertically integrated truck manufacturers who didn't want to buy from independents even if their products performed satisfactorily.

Shifted in 1966 from vice president of finance (making way for John T. Hackett), Henry B. Schacht was put in charge of Europe and would explain: the oversquares "didn't work—they weren't anywhere near developed. We had decided to leapfrog a new technology, which was very unusual, and very risky, and it cost us a bloody fortune. Those engines were a bloody catastrophe."[7] Their manufacture would cease in 1967/68.

Miller shouldn't shoulder the entire blame. Lacking training and on-the-job experience in engine technology, he had let himself be guided by his chief engineer, Nev Reiners, "Father of the V Engines," the epithet used by the authors of *The Engine That Could*.[8] But Miller wasn't comfortable pinning the debacle on Reiners. He "retained his faith in Reiners long after others in the organization had begun looking elsewhere for technical leadership."[9] And while Miller loathed firing people,[10] an automobile accident late in 1964 ended Reiner's career anyhow. R&E leadership would remain unsteady, however, as four different men would head this indispensable activity between 1965 and 1972.[11]

Another major fiasco of the early sixties was a proposed merger with White Motor Company. It was a terrible mistake by Miller that might have resulted in disaster for Cummins and its shareholders.

In April of 1960, Cummins's management "initiated serious conversation about a combination with White."[12] After much analysis and many meetings, the two companies announced their intention to merge more than three years later in September 1963.

Based in Cleveland, Ohio, White was America's second-largest heavy-duty truck producer, with 24 percent of the market in 1962, just behind the leader, Mack Truck, at 25 percent. White sourced 100 percent of its heavy-duty diesels from Cummins, and thus White was Cummins's biggest customer and Cummins, White's biggest supplier. White had recently purchased several smaller truck makers, and three non–truck engine businesses. Its sales, accordingly, had soared from $167 million in 1953 to $447 million in 1963, so White was near triple the size of Cummins, which that year had had revenues of $167 million.[13]

What White wanted was to make its own heavy-duty engines, like its archcompetitors, Mack and General Motors. What Cummins sought was protection against vertical integration by customers like White. At the time, Cummins profits were almost entirely dependent on the NH truck engine.

Cummins, interestingly, was much more profitable than White. It had netted $10.6 million in 1962. According to *Businessweek*, this was "not very far from the $12 million White earned on three times the volume."[14] Cummins's shareholders were to get 50.9 percent and White's 49.1 percent in the proposed White-Cummins Corporation.

Miller obviously approved of the deal, or he wouldn't have agreed. Although he and his family would probably need to move to Chicago (chosen as headquarters for the new corporation), he would be the chairman and the chief executive officer, and he and his family would be the largest shareholders in the new company, owning 30 percent of the stock (down from 63 percent in Cummins alone).[15]

Many constituents, however, were dismayed by the proposed deal. The authors of *The Engine That Could* (Cummins's sponsored history) wrote, "Nearly three years of hard work [resulted in] a group of confused stockholders, an agitated distributor network, and a reservoir of suspicion among most of the company's key customers."[16] From our vantage point, the deal looked like a disaster to come. White likely would have laid waste to anything of Cummins other than the NH engine, and it would spook off other OEMs buying the NH.

In any event, the merger would have to first be approved by the US Department of Justice, headed by Robert F. Kennedy, brother of the recently assassinated president John F. Kennedy. But weeks and then months passed with no word from Washington. Miller's son Will recalls that his father

> had a low opinion of Bobby Kennedy because whenever the Kennedys needed his help [e.g., on civil rights, in his role as Lay President of the National Council of Churches], Bobby regularly called him and asked for it. Dad always did what was asked. But when Dad needed to have a conversation with Bobby in his role as

Attorney General about where the Justice Department stood on the White-Cummins merger, Bobby never returned his calls. Dad did not have much respect for Bobby's decision to avoid having to make a difficult political decision by simply refusing to even engage in a conversation.[17]

Laurie Hoagland, of Irwin Management, recalls Miller was "frosted."[18]

It turns out that Bobby Kennedy inadvertently did Cummins a huge favor. Subsequent events showed that a merger with White would have been a disaster. Will says his father never would have liked moving to Chicago. "The White Board of Directors turned out to be full of people whose values would have been 'out of synch' with Dad's and Cummins'. In all likelihood, Cummins senior management, including Dad, would have been forced out of the merged company within a few years and the whole thing would have gone downhill,"[19] as did White, per se. Unable to enter the heavy-duty engine business by merging with Cummins, White decided to build its own motors. In rapid succession, it created a research center in California, up-fitted a foundry in Iowa and an assembly plant in Ohio—and went bankrupt in four years. Although the deal never happened, countless man-years of staff, attorneys, and consultants were involved.

The attempt to merge with White actually came on the heels of two smaller acquisitions that were of dubious grounds and, in our opinion, should not have happened—an iron foundry in South Bend, Indiana (owned by Studebaker, it was tooled for high production of small parts, not low-volume production of large components), and a manufacturer of car and truck air conditioners—Frigiking that had little connection with engines. The foundry, never profitable, was shuttered, and Frigiking, a marginal moneymaker, was sold in the early seventies.

Cummins in the 1960s would not meet the targets laid down by Miller in his speech at year-end 1961. But its profits more than tripled.

Cummins' Performance (Millions)

	1960 base	1970 target	1970 actual
Sales	$136	$540	$449
Profit	6	30	20

Cummins had dodged a bullet, but changes were still needed.

The failure of the oversquare V engine, in particular, caused Miller to decide that research and engineering could no longer be crammed in close quarters with manufacturing but deserved its own expanded and upgraded space, so in March 1963, he disclosed plans to erect a new, separate R&E facility for occupancy in late 1967 across Hawcreek from Plant #1.

"We are building the most important diesel research center in the world," he declared in a speech later that year. "We mean business. We mean never again to have to respond to a competitor's development. We mean to… be out first with a product so clearly superior in economy, bulk, weight and long life that our excellence does not have to be argued."[20] We imagine Miller would burrow deep into the details of this project—it was the largest capital undertaking in company history.

In a 1968 *Fortune* magazine interview, Miller said that he "sees the company successfully passing through a transition period from seat-of-the-pants technology to a more elaborate scientific approach." With its new $23 million research center, Miller said, "All current engines are potentially obsolete, because now we can lay down all the parameters of a customer's requirements and produce the engine he needs at great savings."[21] Never saying something he didn't mean, Miller boils down the design, development, and production of a new engine to a terribly oversimplified process.

While *Fortune* reported that "top executives hint that Cummins is close to a breakthrough that will make existing diesels obsolete" (a turbine engine, they speculated), it wrote, "If Cummins has its way, it will forestall the introduction of turbine engines by producing a diesel that will be especially light and powerful."

The company would find that neither a sophisticated, state-of-the-art research center nor super-smart, worldly-wise, nontechnical additions to the board of directors would create, per se, breakthrough new engine products. In fact, in that decade of the 1960s, Cummins would produce only one successful new engine domestically—the V903, a heavy-duty V built at Plant #1. But due to its weight versus its size, it never captured significant sales beyond the US military.

In the 1970s, Cummins's only new engine product was the K, "not substantially larger that the NH... [it] had a displacement, that was approximately one-third greater."[22]

Despite the challenges, Miller was also determined to get Cummins listed on the New York Stock Exchange. The failure to conform to requirements for outside directors[23] (the company had none in 1963) caused Miller to recruit and appoint over the next two years five noncompany people of unquestioned integrity and noted accomplishment, likely patterned after the practices of the Yale Corporation and the Ford Foundation.[24] These were men of the Eastern establishment, the likes with whom he mingled on his new boards as well as at New York City's prestigious men's club, the Links, that he'd just joined: in 1964, Eugene R. Black, former president of the World Bank; Harold H. Helms, chairman of Chemical Bank New York Trust; Henry L. Hillman, chairman and president of Pittsburgh Coke & Chemical; Paul L. Miller, president of First Boston; and, in 1965, James B. Fisk, president of Bell Telephone Laboratories (a subsidiary of AT&T on whose board Miller sat).[25] Despite an abundance of staff helping in Columbus, selecting and recruiting this unique group of outside directors had to have taken a good deal of Miller's time between 1963 and 1965.

Luckily, Cummins, as a company, had brought to market many types of diesel engines in its fifty-year existence. Thus, less fuel efficient than the NH, the K, launched during the Middle East war that sent fuel cost soaring, was relegated to niche markets, such as line-haul trucks running through mountainous terrain.

Emblematic of the enormous ingenuity, effort, and just plain luck in development of new diesels, two stand out as game changers—way beyond the others—but just two: the NH, introduced in 1945 (and fitted with the PT fuel pump in 1954) was the flagship into the 1980s; and the B, launched in 1983, which became the flagship into the twenty-first century. The NH was the first, heavy duty at 14 liters, the second, medium duty at 5.9 liters. Both in-line 6-cylinder.

While later we will see how the B engine saved the company in the 1990s, the NH drove Cummins's fortunes from the 1950s through the 1980s. Sadly, the two protagonists that created these engines—Clessie L. Cummins, the NH (and PT), and Phillip E. Jones, the B—received neither the credit nor respect they deserved in their lifetimes. It seems Miller himself underestimated the rarity of creating something like the Clessie Cummins NH engine—and the horrendous odds against developing another engine with the NH's impact more than once in a generation. The NH carried the engine company through three decades.

Successor to the H introduced in the 1920s, the NH was launched in 1945 (as seen), the PT in 1954. The PT (for progressive timing) was "a direct injection system in which fuel circulated continuously and injection was timed mechanically by a plunger activated by the camshaft."[26] The PT, as already narrated, was thought to give Cummins Engine a twenty-year advantage vis-à-vis its competition.[27] It not only performed admirably but involved many fewer parts and was thus cheaper to build.

Cummins was back on track despite its CEO devoting substantial amounts of time to two civil rights causes he'd committed to and his company facing a host of problems of its own creation. On the back of the nonpareil NH engine, Cummins Engine was slingshot through the sixties and seventies, its sales climbing near 250 percent in each of these decades as seen in the table below, the greatest growth in its history.

Cummins Performance[28]

Years	Sales(Mills)	Growth Rate
1951–1960	$61–136	123%
1961–1970	129–449	248
1971–1980	492–1,667	239
1981–1990	1,962–3,462	76
1991–2000	3,406–6,597	94
2001–2010	5,681–13,226	133

It went from a single factory in Columbus in 1956 to eleven factories worldwide by 1967, making in-house components like crankshafts and turbochargers and operating worldwide, including a plant in Australia, a licensee in Japan, and a joint venture in India. Profits, excepting a dip during a broad economic weakness in 1967, climbed year after year and would more than triple (actually grow 3.3 times) during the decade. And the engine company would triple its profits again in the decade of the 1970s on the back of the NH.

It was a testimony to the long shadow Clessie Cummins cast over his namesake company: of the 160,000 engines that Cummins sold worldwide in 1979, 124,000 were NHs—that's 78 percent (and the engine was thirty-four years old!). Including parts, NH sales would have to have been over 90 percent of total revenues, and, including parts business, in total, account for 100 percent of profits (maybe more given those losing businesses).

Thank goodness for Clessie!

Meanwhile, Miller was cutting back his extracurricular pursuits. He resigned from the boards of both Butler University and Equitable Life Insurance in 1964, the year of completion of North Christian Church's construction that he would no longer have to coax along. And he stepped down as chairman of the board of CTS (per its bylaws) in 1965.[29]

Before the decade ended, Miller had sold the venerable Union Starch and Refining Company (to Miles Laboratories) and liquidated the family's holdings in Purity Stores, the California grocery chain, leaving Irwin Management and Irwin Union Bank as the surviving Irwin-Sweeney-Miller businesses, alongside the engine company.

In May 1966, he penned a handwritten list of his pro bono responsibilities with his thoughts on what to do about each. Some of these notes we reckon are simply musings as, for example, he never did cut back to "half meetings" at his alma mater. According to Sam Chauncey, chief of staff, who had reason to know, Miller would attend every meeting of the Yale Corporation right to the end of his tenure.[30]

Butler   Resign   ok
CTS   Stay off   ok
NCC   Stay off   ok
WCC   Attend Central Council. ok   → no Purity meetings
                Postpone CCIA ok
Equitable   Resign   ok
Chemical >   Talk (half)
AT+T
Ford F.   half meetings (call Mac B-)
Yale   no more chairman / half · meetings

2 Govt Comm Resign
no speeches for 1 year.

Embargo Review ?

① Can't omit ≠ Cummins meetings

② Can't omit   Trips overseas

③ Kids —

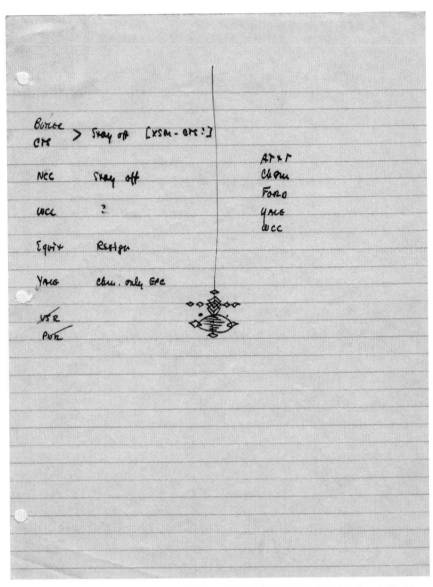

Business and pro-bono commitments crowded Miller's calendar in 1965.
Provided by the Indiana Historical Society

11

Miller for President?

In December 1963, a month after the assassination of John F. Kennedy, John Cowles, editor of the *Star and Tribune* of Minneapolis, wrote to Miller, asking him if he "would have the slightest interest in having your name tossed into the political ring as a one in a million Presidential long-shot?"[1] Miller replied, "It would be arrogant, embarrassing, and the height of folly even to start entertaining such notions: so the answer is an unqualified no."[2]

Four years later, *Esquire* magazine ran a cover story on Miller with a provocative cover line that read, "This man ought to be the next president of the United States." Inside, the article asks rhetorically, "Is it too late for a man of honesty, high purpose and intelligence to be elected President of the United States in 1968?"[3]

Again demurring, Miller stated, "I'm not a candidate. And that's not because I despise politics. I have a great admiration for men who have the capacity to go through the election process and I know myself well enough to know I'm not that kind of a guy."[4]

When he was interviewed by the author, Lee Hamilton, a seventeen-term Congressman from southern Indiana (1964–1998), said, "Miller was a towering figure and deeply respected for so many causes. He had enormous interest in politics… yet he knew he wasn't cut out for politics and should not have been President… He was an intellectual, cordial but not effusive… He was aloof with the average person, not a back-slapper… He didn't react quickly like a politician and was not a very good speaker."[5]

And, indeed, Miller always paid very close attention to politics. In the *Esquire* story, he acknowledged

> a consuming interest in politics, which also comes from his father. Hugh Thomas Miller had been a professor of history and languages at Butler University in Indianapolis... he later was elected Lieutenant Governor of Indiana. In 1914, he was nominated for the Senate and defeated. He planned to run again for the other Senate seat in the 1916 election, but had to withdraw because of a siege of tuberculosis.

> Miller imbibed the tenets of Republicanism, although... he has not hesitated to turn against the party when it nominated a man like Barry Goldwater, but he believes party affiliation is important."

> He declared, "I don't really believe in being independent. I think the place of influence is in the primary and in the election of the candidate... no political party is going to please you 100 percent or even very much of the time, so you pick the party that outrages you the least."[6]

> Periodically, he would reassert that "I am a lifelong Republican."[7]

The Irwin-Sweeney-Miller collection at the Indiana Historical Society only occasionally helps identify Miller's choice in presidential elections. Reaching voting age in 1930, or two years before Franklin D. Roosevelt was first elected president, it is highly likely that Miller was taking his cue from his great-uncle W. G. Irwin, patriarch of the family mansion on Fifth Street, who was a delegate to six straight Republican National Conventions from 1916 through 1936.[8]

Miller probably voted for Roosevelt in 1932, but maybe not in 1936. Years later, Miller recalled "Unc was enchanted by FDR the first 100 days, but 'packing' the Supreme Court he thought was unethical," and lost his enthusiasm.[9]

Miller assuredly backed Wendell L. Willkie, a Hoosier native, picked as the GOP's standard bearer in 1940. Not only did Miller and his sister, Clementine, attend that summer's convention in Philadelphia, but also they sat alongside Mrs. Willkie.[10]

Miller's disdain of FDR continued. Returned from the war in 1944 at the end of FDR's third term, he wrote his sister, "I don't like Mr. Roosevelt's vindictiveness, his smear tactics, his terrible neglect of the domestic situation, including his blind handling of the labor situation which has set the cause of labor back another ten to twenty years."[11]

Just before the election, Miller told her, "[Roosevelt] heads a bankrupt party in that they have no leadership to offer save his after twelve years; it is a worn-out party... it is a corrupt party... it is a class party... On the other hand, Mr. [Thomas E.] Dewey is a disappointment... [with] no personal ideas, ideals or goals, except to win. He tailors his talk strictly for votes. I never felt that Willkie did... In other words, I do not want to vote for either Dewey or Roosevelt."[12]

On November 25, 1944, with the election over, Miller wrote Clementine, "I wobbled from side to side during the campaign, and finally voted for Roosevelt (the family does not definitely know this)... I will trust Roosevelt to do better with the peace than Dewey."[13]

Though the ISM collection contains no hint of his views on Harry S. Truman, elected president in 1948 after succeeding to the office in 1945 upon the death of FDR, Miller presumably voted twice for Dwight D. Eisenhower in 1952 and 1956, as he wrote about "the constructive efforts of [Ike's] administration,"[14] alluding to the start of work on the federal highway system which spurred demand for Cummins products.

It appears that Miller voted for Richard M. Nixon in 1960—he received a thankyou note for his contribution of $334.[15] If so, it was possibly more of a vote against the winner, John F. Kennedy, who might have drawn Miller's disdain by his elitism, womanizing, and/or Catholicism.

And then, a thousand days later, Kennedy was assassinated amid sharply rising domestic tension stemming from civil rights unrest and Vietnam War opposition, and Vice President Lyndon B. Johnson became president and Democratic front-runner for the 1964 presidential election. This marks a shift in Miller's allegiances. Miller's apparent drift to the Democrats in presidential politics is mirrored and nurtured by his mounting concern that American society is getting into deeper and deeper trouble.

Still reflecting his Republican roots but appalled by the GOP's choice of Barry Goldwater, Miller initially supports New York governor Nelson Rockefeller (who quickly backs out) and then Pennsylvania governor William Scranton (who also does a fast fade), so he decides to vote for the Democrats, sending Johnson a check for $1,000.[16]

On January 5, 1965, just before the start of LBJ's second swearing in, Miller writes Johnson, "Although I am a lifelong Republican, you have charted a specific course for this nation which arouses my enthusiasm more than that set out by any President in my lifetime."[17] Miller would give LBJ not just money but, more dearly, his time.

At the request of President Lyndon B. Johnson, Miller served on four special federal committees between 1964 and 1968, the first two as chairman: US trade relations with Eastern Europe and Russia; health manpower needs; reorganization of the US Post Office; and urban housing.[18]

Of course, Miller would bring help with him from Columbus: James A. Henderson (future president of Cummins), on East-West trade; Talmadge G. Rogers, on health manpower and postal reorganization; and Philip Sorenson on urban housing. The committees themselves consisted typically of executives of leading American companies (e.g., Caterpillar Tractor, Deere & Co., E. I. DuPont, General Foods, and Chase Manhattan Bank).

Miller evidently took these committee assignments very seriously, especially East-West trade, from mid-1964 to the end of 1965. William Blackie, chairman of Caterpillar, called this group the "Miller Committee." Another member, Herman B. Wells, chancellor of Indiana University, wrote Miller, "I was filled with admiration with the way you organized the work and drove it through. I have never seen a better committee performance, and I have spent about three-fourths of my life on committees."[19] And Art Goldfinger, director of the Department of Research, AFL/CIO Unions, wrote, "You were a completely fair Chairman, as well as a strong one, who succeeded in getting a tremendous volume of work done in a very brief period of time."[20]

In January of 1966, Miller wrote Johnson, "I was most pleased that you asked in your 'State of the Union' message for power to... expand trade between the United States and Eastern Europe and the Soviet Union... Each of us... on your committee [was] convinced of the importance of the task you had assigned us." In reply, Johnson called the Committee's work "a fine report."[21] Evidently delighted with Miller's leadership on East-West trade, Johnson, a bit more than a year later (April 10, 1967), appoints Miller to head a "special panel to determine if the Post Office should be reorganized as a non-cabinet federal corporation."[22]

Regarding his decision to chair another committee again, Miller wrote his Congressman, Lee Hamilton: "I was reluctant to accept an appointment... to study the Post Office Department because I have got more than I can do justice to at the present time. However, my interest in the department is very great. The importance of the job is obviously tremendous, and so I found it difficult to decline."[23]

With LBJ giving way to Hubert H. Humphrey in 1968, Miller falls back into party lines. Despite the manifold demands for his time, Miller runs the nationwide campaign for the reemerging Rockefeller.[24] But it gains insufficient traction (Jim Henderson was assigned for a year to help manage this process).[25] Likely, due to his usual proclivity toward the Republicans, Miller sends Nixon another check for $3,000.[26]

In 1971, Miller finances the presidential campaign of John V. Lindsay, New York City's mayor, who switches his party affiliation from Republican to Democrat. Lindsay, however, runs a poor fifth in the Florida primary in spring of 1972 and pulls out of the race. Nixon beats Hubert Humphrey to gain a second term and puts Miller on his "enemies list."[27]

Nixon viewed Miller as a radical. Between 1969 and 1973, the Cummins Engine Foundation appointed full-time officers to represent the black community in five major American cities, providing financial support to minorities. One example was the $20,000 grant given to the Afro-American Patrolmen's League in Chicago, which comprised three thousand black officers. As Miller also intended, the field officer's program exposed the managers of Cummins to the realities of the black urban experience.[28]

The ISM collection has no data about Miller's preference in the 1976 election (when Jimmy Carter beat Gerald Ford), but when Carter runs against Ronald Reagan in 1980, Miller writes, "I will sit this one out—I have no enthusiasm whatever for Jimmy Carter, but [am] scared to death of Reagan. His simplistic answers to complex questions make no sense."[29]

Much later, in regard to William J. Clinton's victory in 1992 over Reagan's vice president, George H. W. Bush, Miller wrote the following autumn, "I still bet that [Clinton] will probably do well at the horribly difficult job which faces him. It is ironic (and shameful) that the Republicans, who made the present mess, now seem to get so much joy out of taking pot-shots at the first person who has tried to clean it up."[30] (This letter is the last on presidential elections that the author could find in the ISM collection.) There is plenty of evidence that Miller's political views in the last third of his life became more leftist (or, as it was more commonly known back then, "socialistic").

Miller remained passionate about the direction our country was headed, but began assuming a leadership role, rather than that of an activist, as he did sitting on so many outside boards. In 1971, he wrote a Providence banker, "I am convinced that we need to lower our private standard of living in order to achieve an acceptable public standard of living."[31] That same year he said in an address dedicating new offices for the *Republic*: "In a society of abundance the survival of those on top of the pile will very probably hang upon their ability to accomplish changes in systems and equitable redistribution of our new wealth such that no doors of opportunity are closed to any American simply by reason of where he was born, or how much money his parents had, or because of his race or his religion."[32]

In 1973, in a lecture at Northwestern University, Miller said, "Our commitment to equality now becomes pretty feeble," and he calls for "a substantial tax increase."[33] A final example, in a speech to the Rotary Club of Columbus in 1993, called "Service above Self," Miller advocated "more taxes paid now by you and me… in an amount which will reduce at least somewhat our present standard of living. The mantle of service has a beautiful shining exterior but the lining of that garment is uncomfortable, and always prickly to the touch. No one wears it happily, though we are delighted for the other fellow to put it on."[34]

He would continue, though, to wield great influence in the decades to come.

IV

12

Stepping Down... But Not Out

In the summer of 1968, Miller, now fifty-nine years-old, felt it was time to hand over day-to-day decision making at Cummins to a worthy successor. He had been CEO and chairman of the board for eighteen years. Also, Miller's number two, president and COO E. Donald Tull, was "in poor health and failing noticeably."[1]

Miller asked Cummins vice president of management development James A. ("Jim") Henderson and director of personnel Theodore L. ("Ted") Marston for their views on "management changes needed at the top of the company." Marston and Henderson responded that "the best qualified man in the company to be its next President was current Executive Vice-President and Corporate General Manager, Richard B. Stoner." Further, they added, vice president of manufacturing Vaughn L. Beals is "the most qualified for Chief Operating Officer."[2]

On a Saturday that November (presumably in his office at 301 Washington Street, felt pen clutched in his left hand), Miller set down his thoughts on succession in a seven page memo (labeled "discuss with [Donald Tull]") and also concluded that Dick Stoner was, in fact, the best man to be the next president of the engine company. Indeed, wrote Miller, he is the "only candidate" (see appendage later in this chapter).[3]

But Miller had also thrown another name into the mix—Henry B. Schacht. And, on a numerical basis weighing four criteria (experience in finance, personnel, new business negotiation, and planning), Schacht is rated a nine—the same as Stoner. Curiously, Miller appears to have let drift the decision on the next president for some months, and there is no evidence in the ISM collection of correspondence with his five new outside directors on this important subject. But the next spring (April, it appears), Miller again addresses the matter of succession. "We believe company should choose now a new President," he penned in another handwritten memo,

> Because (a) job of... is Physically demanding, precludes maximum outside involvement, Has changed in character-requires new style-much greater reliance on continuous planning, use of greatly increased information, and delegation Management of distant enterprises, (b) This dictates a young man-in our opinion-preferably 40 or less. Business conditions changed significantly about 10 years ago. Those who were executives prior to that time have great difficulties with the kind of change required.[4]

Interestingly, Miller's singling out youth as an essential criterion is further understood in the context of a letter he would write a couple of years later regarding selection of a new president for Christian Theological Seminary:

> The candidate certainly ought to be young. By "young" I mean preferably around 35. There is a reason for saying this. I have found... that if a person has accumulated a great deal of "experience", he makes his plans and programs based on the lessons of that experience. An older person, mid-forties to mid-fifties has gained his experience in a world that no longer exists.[5]

Given this emphatic point of view regarding age, Miller suddenly drops Stoner, age forty-nine, from consideration and shifts his focus to his two other key line executives—Beals, age thirty-seven, and Schacht, age thirty-five.

Miller rates the two men as equal in regards to education, experience, leadership, and intelligence. But in terms of sensitivity to people and creativity, he gives Schacht a distinctive edge (a copy of Miller's one-page analysis appears below). Garnett Keith, who worked at Irwin Management from 1963 to 1977 (later becoming a top executive at Prudential Insurance) states, "Miller believed a good manager could run any business… Hank had the mind. He could deal with Miller as an equal."[6]

Miller directed that the announcement of Schacht's promotion be made after May 1 and that the board of directors would vote all changes at a special meeting midJune in New York City. Importantly, he also ruminates "are we going to lose anyone? Probably [Stoner] after 2 years [though, Stoner ended up staying until he reached retirement]; less probably VLB [Vaughn L. Beals]." (Beals actually left in four months and went on to an illustrious career at motorcycle maker Harley-Davidson, not just salvaging it from extinction but also turning it into a first-class company.)

Thanks to an academic paper written by a professor at Harvard Business School, this seemingly straightforward path of transition was dubbed a "relay race," as opposed to a perhaps more typical case where the candidates for corporate office (two or more) vie in an unpredictably (thus sometimes dysfunctional) "horse race."[7]

In 1974, Miller also ceded his CEO title to Henry Schacht (vice president Henderson is made president and COO). And by 1977, Miller held only a largely symbolic role as chairman of the executive committee. Though, as with everything he was involved with, his influence would loom large for years to come.

①

	VLB	HBS
EDUCATION	*Excellent*	*Excellent*
EXPERIENCE	2 yrs - head of R+E: Excellent Result 1½ - " " MFG: First Class progress. Good planner. Stable operator	2 yrs: VP Finance 2 yrs: VP International 1 yr: VP " + SUBS. Outstanding Result with troubled operation
LEADERSHIP	Commands respect. Fully in charge	Commands respect. Fully in charge.
INTELLIGENCE	Outstanding. Goes very deep in analysis. Good (born) planner.	Outstanding.
SENSITIVITY to PEOPLE	Not great. Had difficulties in bargaining. Can learn. Slow to fire.	Instinctively sensitive. Selects, handles people well.
CREATIVITY	Proceeds deliberately. Intuition does not play large part in decisions.	A generalist. Sense of where to man. SOCIAL CONCERN.

In 1969, Miller followed a methodical process, as shown in this document, to choose his successor as CEO of Cummins Engine.
Provided by the Indiana Historical Society

The appointment of Schacht ushered in an interesting time for Cummins and its leadership. Many would agree that during the 1980s and 1990s, Cummins was *not* a well-run company—and that Miller's overly trusting attitude toward hiring was partly to blame.

To Miller, when looking for a leader, the single most important criterion was character. By character, he meant the innate habit of treating others the way you want them to treat you. We have already seen that sensitivity to people was the tie-breaker in his selection of Schacht over Vaughn Beals as his successor—the former "instinctively sensitive; selects, handles people well," the latter "not instinctively great, had difficulties in bargaining."[8] In this regard, Jim Henderson told us, "[Miller] didn't want senior officers to be engineers... [he] wanted liberal arts... to decide what's right, what's fair."[9]

Buttressing his confidence that character was the number-one criterion in selecting leaders was Miller's absolute conviction that the engine company would eventually prosper, despite terrible years, even terrible decades, owing to the innate ability of its employees to develop profitable products that customers wanted. In this sense, Miller's vision for Cummins aligns neatly with Jim Collins's description in *Good to Great* of excellent companies being like "hedgehogs—simple dowdy creatures that know 'one big thing' and stick to it."[10] Jim Henderson told us that Miller "thought Cummins could do anything if you pushed hard enough. "His focus was on outcome, not process... He couldn't care less about systems."[11]

For the rest of his career, Miller would hold up character as the prime criterion for hiring and promoting people, outstripping experience and knowledge. In a transcribed interview by professor Richard F. Vancil of the Harvard Business School in 1986, Miller and Schacht recount matter-of-factly how Cummins hired Michael D. Walsh, a California district attorney (with no business experience) as international vice president, promoted him quickly to vice president of operations, and elected him a director. In turn, Walsh recruited a lawyer friend, Harris Wagenseil, as vice president of sales when both probably had little notion of business and certainly no knowledge of diesel engines. Yet,

Cummins's top management (presumably backed by its board) had put Walsh on the fast track ("the relay race") to succeed Henderson as president (Schacht noted that Walsh was eight years younger—"which is just about the right differential for our current situation," Miller noted).[12]

Walsh left Cummins later that year to become CEO of the Union Pacific Railroad. Not before, however (and presumably with the blessing of the company's top management), Walsh personally handled the demotion and "early retirement" of Phil Jones, that outspoken Liverpudlian from Perkins who fathered the B and C engines and thus probably ranked second only to Clessie Cummins in terms of design engineering over the company's history. Without the B, Cummins Engine probably would not have lasted until the twenty-first century.

In 1987 at Cummins's annual planning conference, Miller (then seventy-eight) spoke about leadership. He said, "It is a lifetime habit and finally the unconscious practice of dealing with those for whom you are responsible and those with whom you work in the way you wish your boss would deal with you, in the way you wish your associates would work with you."

Miller added six outside directors in the 1970s. Like the people chosen in the 1960s, they were uncommon individuals (including two minorities) that, in sum, likely constituted the most prestigious corporate board in America during that time.

- 1973: Franklin B. Thomas, president, Bedford Stuyvesant Restoration Corp.; later, president, the Ford Foundation (retired 2003)
- 1974: William D. Ruckelshaus, former EPA administrator and US attorney general (retired 2000)
- Donald B. Perkins, chairman, Jewel Companies (retired 2000)
- Sir William R. Hawthorne, professor, University of Cambridge (retired 1998)
- 1977: Hannah H. Gray, president, University of Chicago (retired 1998)

- William W. Scranton, former governor of Pennsylvania and US ambassador to the United Nations (retired 1998)[13]

The ISM collection has no board of directors' minutes or official correspondence which, logically, repose in the files of Cummins Inc. Again, given Miller's overriding criterion for selecting people being character, one might overlook the facts that just two of Cummins's directors—Hillman and Perkins—came from the corporate world. Only one—Hawthorne—had an engineering background. Nobody had manufacturing experience.

A good deal of the technical material must have baffled them— Perkins said attending engineering sessions was "like playing three-dimensional chess."[14]

One would have to assume that board meetings were well attended—there was usually a round of golf or two; Cummins fetched and delivered directors in its airplanes; and chef Jim Gregory prepared first-class meals. One meeting per year (typically) was held at an overseas plant (with wives invited too), and, as acknowledged, the directors were an unusually diverse, accomplished, well-connected, bright bunch of people. Likely, one dinner was held at 2760 Highland Way with its six gorgeous impressionist paintings and small Henry Moore sculpture.[15] Miller might have even played his violin.

There seems to have been a tremendous current of goodwill back and forth between Miller and his board. As example, Bill Scranton writes to proffer his retirement in the fall of 1987, "a very difficult decision because of the outstanding persons one meets and gets to know in the Cummins group... any good director could spend all of his or her time at Cummins just learning a great deal from so many high-calibered people." And in his remarks at Scranton's retirement dinner the spring of 1988, Miller said, "He has been Director, Governor, Congressman, Bank Chairman and ought to have been President... He is one of only two persons in this room who has fitted into and gone down the slide at The Commons playground... To us your name is Moses, and without you steadily at our side we are less sure we will reach the Promised Land."[16]

And then there are Miller's laudatory words about Henry Hillman at his retirement dinner on April 1, 1991:

> Henry, who well may be America's most prized Director, remained timeless and committed to the service of the company... Henry stuck with us and encouraged Hank and Jim as they aggressively pursued our common vision... I can count at least six great efforts and six equally great failures, but I can also say that we have now got there, and without Henry Hillman's advocacy and encouragement and belief, the road would have gotten many times harder, indeed... Cummins has had no Director so committed, so tactfully outspoken, so persuasive, so thoughtful... He is one of America's great corporate directors.[17]

While the Cummins board meetings had to have been among the most interesting, fun activities of its directors, the company itself was not headed in the right direction. Profits were up, but it was far from a smooth ride—the process could be described as brute strength and awkwardness.

As we've seen, launching new products continued as the absolute top priority of the company after the debacle of the oversquare Vs. First came the V903 in 1967, also a V but a heavy-duty engine that enjoyed fair usage by the US military but not much elsewhere. Next, in 1973, came the K, an in-line six like the NH but somewhat larger, less fuel efficient (during time of rising cost), and relegated mainly to niche industrial applications. And then, in 1982, the L10 (for ten liter) that found usage in buses, as example. Finally, came the B, launched in 1983 (and the C in 1984), which opened up to Cummins the vast market for small diesels but produced losses into the mid-1990s.

Fortuitously, other than the V903, the new engines were not built in Columbus—the K, Charleston, South Carolina; the L10, Jamestown,

New York; and the B and C, Rocky Mount, North Carolina. Thus, venerable Plant #1 could focus on producing the NH.

Having chosen Hank Schacht to succeed him as president the previous July, Miller named Jim Henderson as vice president of operations in February 1970, even though he had no operating experience.[18] Schacht and Henderson, sensing strong, continuous demand for the NH, immediately undertook major capital expenditures. A major investment was at Plant #1, a transfer line from Ingersoll Milling Machine to make cylinder blocks (the name "transfer" signifying castings were moved by conveyor from station to station). Another large expenditure was at Walesboro, a town twelve miles south of Columbus, a 563,000-square-foot facility to house a variety of machine lines moved from Plant #1.

Problems with these two projects arose almost immediately. The transfer line was found incapable of machining the volumes needed, and Cummins, on a crash basis, had to enlarge Plant #1 by 60,000 square feet and reinstall the old, worn machine tools to supplement output from the Ingersoll line. And, as regards Walesboro, "the new components plant suffered from low productivity, vandalism, and 'negative climate' almost as soon as it opened."[19]

Even with these major capital projects, Cummins "simply had miscalculated the potential for growth in the heavy-duty truck business."[20] And it spent nearly eight years in the 1970s on allocation.[21] However, there was one ironic advantage: Cummins had to abandon its nonengine diversification strategy (the so-called "three-legged stool"), which Miller disliked, anyway, to husband capital for the core business.

A fifty-seven-day strike at southern Indiana plants in 1972, deeply upsetting Miller, shattered any illusions this was Clessie Cummins's workforce—after all, many of them were the children and grandchildren of Linnie Sweeney's "trade school," expecting to graduate from high school and to work at the engine company until retirement.

As a member of manufacturing management at Plant #1 and Walesboro, in the late 1970s, the author saw firsthand what was happening. Deriving from the stated initial purpose of the company to provide jobs, Cummins made nearly everything in-house, including push rods. It offered its customers most anything they asked for, as example, over one thousand different types of flywheels.[22] The unions were adamantly opposed to outsourcing and were complicit in making people slow their work pace.

Reflecting insufficient manufacturing engineering, machining processes were suspect. Five- to six-thousand cylinder blocks typically awaited "salvage"—ten to twelve days' production. Also, an entire department had been created for a dozen or so newfangled numerically controlled machine tools, permitting rapid changeover from part number to part number and optimal build, but most of the NC equipment ran the same part number for days, if not weeks.

While the concept of material requirements planning (or MRP) was accepted by most American companies, it required accurate part counts. "By the early 1970s, Cummins was not exactly sure what it had in inventory or where it was."[23] Consequently, production control people usually made a physical count each day, part number by part number.

Miller knew full well what was going on at his engine company. In a letter to Henderson, copy to Schacht, on March 19, 1981, he wrote the following:

> I stopped in unannounced at the Case/Cummins Center on 14th Street,[24] and was really shocked at the dirty conditions… and at the appearance of no work whatsoever going on. There were groups of people standing around; there was little or no activity in test cells. When one thinks… that we will go into full production of (the engine families) in a very short number of years; that, if these engines are not virtually perfect, the failure to perform in terms of cash loss, as well as market loss, will be enormous, then I can say only that I am very worried indeed… This is one of the saddest outfits I have ever seen. The contrast between this visit and previous visits where they were prepared for us is embarrassing, and kind of cynical. Why dress

in white coats for bosses' visits, and dirty jeans and unshaven faces the rest of the time? Also, why spend money on landscaping and architecture when it will be treated as an unsupervised pig pen?[25]

Later that summer, he offered his views on the company's mainstay, heavy-duty operation in the Columbus area (a letter to Henderson, with copies to Schacht, Marston, and Tull):

Our irrelevant standards of hiring have admitted persons not up to the standards Cummins needs… a real concern to me is slow work pace—for which we have long been famous. People who have time on their hands can slip away to Paul's Café during working hours and never be missed. Of course, we have stopped that by locking the gates, but a better way would be to require a fair day's work for fair pay. Under such conditions there is no way a fellow could slip out without being missed.

S. L. Kirloskar's daughter[26] was asked last week for her impressions when she finished her tour of the CEP and Walesboro. She replied, "No productivity." I took a visitor to Walesboro a few months ago in the middle of a shift, and he said, "Why are they all on lunch break at this time of day?" I paid a surprise visit to the Small Engine project at 9:15 a.m. recently. All [sic] were sitting down at tables drinking coffee and cokes. One Saturday afternoon, I visited the NH assembly line at the CEP. They had brought in a TV and all were watching [on overtime] the regional basketball tournament. A current shop employee recently told me. "I have worked many places. No place makes as few demands on it employees for production as Cummins." The community word is "The Cummins Playhouse".[27]

13

Miller's Big Miscalculation

The financial performance of Schacht and Henderson was not nearly as strong as that of either Miller, who preceded them, or Solso, who succeeded them. (See table below; detailed financial statements are appended at the back of this book.) But their legacy at Cummins is far more complicated than that.

Comparison of Cummins's CEOs

Cumulative (Mil)			Net			Years of
Years	#	Incumbent	Sales	Profit	Margin	Losses
1951–77	26	Miller	$9,367	$380	4.1%	0/26
1978–99	21	Schacht/ Henderson	$75,110	$1,138	1.5%	8/21
2000–11	12	Solso	$123,600	$6,510	5.3%	1/12

Many observers think Schacht and Henderson should have been replaced. "I question whether any other corporation would have allowed them to serve in their positions as long as Cummins did," said Tom Shenk, trucking industry executive and former employee of a Cummins distributor.[1] "In normal circumstances, Jim Henderson and Hank Schacht would have been out on their ears," we were told by Donald S. Perkins, former chairman of Jewel Tea and director of Cummins from 1974 to 2000. "They played for long-term because the lead-time to develop new engines... was so long."[2] Fred Reams, former Cummins pension manager, said, "John Hackett [Cummins CFO] kept Henry and Jim from being lunatics... Hank made a lot of mistakes, though he could sell equity to anyone."[3] And needed to, we'd add!

Susan Hanafee, author of *Red, Black and Global*, company-sponsored sequel to *The Engine That Could*, told us, "Hank and Jim were over their heads."[4] Ted Marston, Cummins's vice president of personnel, stated, "Tim Solso turned Cummins around after Schacht and Henderson retired."[5] Jim Henderson himself explained, "It took us so long to take on the Japanese and get the product-line straightened out. I'd have been fired if I'd worked at a lot of other companies."[6]

However, the engine business is a long game, in which results aren't always black and white. First, as Don Perkins noted, diesel engines, even if they survive gestation, take decades to reach maturity. We saw this in the case of the heavy-duty NH, introduced in 1945 and still going strong in 1979, when it commanded 78 percent of Cummins's revenues. It took almost twenty years for the mid-range Bs and Cs (introduced in the early 1980s) to get to 77 percent of Cummins's sales or to become as dominant as heavy duty had been (midrange units climbing from 19 percent to 77 percent, with heavy duty falling from 78 percent to 22 percent—although the absolute numbers grew very significantly).

of Engines Sold by Cummins (000)

	1980	1990	2000
Midrange	30 (19%)	124 (56%)	318 (77%)
Heavy Duty	124 (78%)	81 (36%)	92 (22%)
High Horsepower	6 (3%)	8 (4%)	12 (1%)
Kits		10 (4%)	
Total	160 (100%)[A]	223 (100%)[B]	412 (100%)[C]

Sources:

[A]   *The Engine That Could*, p. 329 (most of midrange in 1980 were small Vs)
[B]   1990 Cummins Annual Report
[C]   2000 Cummins Annual Report

But beyond the phase-out of the NH and the phase-in of the Bs and Cs, there were other exogenous developments in the 1980s which severely compounded the difficulty of running the business: for one, Japanese diesel engine builders, mimicking their car makers, cut prices 30 percent in the United States to try to take over this market. Meanwhile, a recession started in the United States and lasted until the mid-1990s, and Cummins's major domestic rivals, first Caterpillar and then Detroit Diesel, strongly rebounded with new engines. Finally, this was the dawn of strict environmental legislation. The US Environmental Protection Agency (EPA) steadily toughened emissions laws around NOx (oxides of nitrogen) and particulate matter.

In 1984, in a move of absolutely extraordinary courage, Schacht cut Cummins's prices 30 percent across the board without stopping to determine where or when it could take out commensurate cost. And, equally bold, Cummins continued its policy of spending 5 percent of sales on research and engineering (earmarking more and more funds for pollution control).

Importantly, too, reflecting its unbending moral commitment to "do what's right," Cummins continued to "take the high ground." Rather than fight the EPA over emissions standards, Cummins chose to take a nonadversarial role, like a tutor, to help shape regulations that were good for both the environment and Cummins.[7]

Cummins also remained unflinching on civil rights. It was Miller himself who essentially said "Nuts!" to a solicitation by the apartheid government of South Africa in the mid-1980s to build in that country a new diesel engine factory whose purpose, he saw, was "to anticipate sanctions and to have a dependable government-owned supply of diesel engines for [their] police and military, as well as domestic use."[8] Cummins thus abandoned a relatively small, yet highly profitable operation on the basis of its principles.

Cummins attempted to make up the losses by cutting expenses. "More than forty Cummins plants, warehouses and office facilities were closed between 1983 and 1992. Between 1979 and 1989, the Company's southern Indiana shop floor work-force declined from 6,800 to 3,700."[9]

But it wasn't near enough. It lost money six out of seven years between 1986 and 1992.

"We were using capital at a phenomenal rate," recalled the late John T. Hackett. "I wanted to stabilize the company and look at organic growth opportunities. [Schacht] realized I was not supporting his strategy. He was correct. It was time for me to move on. He needed another CFO."[10] Understandably, Hackett was exhausted by trying to find funds to keep the engine company going (the big, new corporate office building in Columbus was financed through a sale-and-leaseback arrangement, for example.)

Cummins paid out dividends greater than its bottom line—earnings or losses—in eight of the ten years from 1982 to 1991, an astonishing lack of governance by Miller and his fellow directors (although their rationale may have been to try to thwart unfriendly takeovers, thinking continuation of dividends would help buoy the share price).

-Per Share-

Year	Earnings (Losses)	Dividends
1982	$0.03	$0.25
1983	0.05	0.25
1984	2.42	0.26
1985	0.65	0.28
1986	(1.31)	0.28
1987	0.07	0.28
1988	(0.84)	0.28
1989	(0.19)	0.28
1990	(1.81)	0.28
1991	(0.62)	0.09

Even worse, Cummins was having huge problems *just paying interest* on its debt. Over the same ten-year stretch, the company's profit *did not* cover interest in two years and covered interest by 1.5 times or less in another six years.

Interest Coverage

Year	
1982	0.1x
1983	0.9
1984	8.3
1985	2.5
1986	(2.9)
1987	1.5
1988	0.2
1989	1.1
1990	(2.0)
1991	0.2

Not surprisingly, the ISM collection does not have minutes of Cummins's board of directors meetings (these we'd suppose are kept in the company vault). However, we can only assume the directors were complicit with the company's dividend decisions. The last two persons who joined the board in the 1960s—Henry L. Hillman and Paul L. Miller—resigned in 1990 and 1991, respectively. Five of the six elected in the 1970s would remain until 1997 or beyond (William Scranton left in 1988). Miller himself would not resign from the board until 1997, at age eighty-eight. But, evidently, he regularly attended meetings through the rest of the decade (although Don Perkins said Miller would not speak during the session).[12]

While debate in Cummins's board meetings was probably lively (and maybe brilliant), this group seemingly deferred to Miller, whose family by the end of the 1980s owned only about 5 percent of the company's shares, which likely would not meet today's corporate governance criteria. "A mutual admiration society" might describe CECo's board.

Perhaps no greater example of Miller putting so much faith in a man was his backing of Henry Schacht, who would eventually leave the company. (Schacht declined being interviewed for this book.)[13]

Though Cummins posted losses in seven of those seventeen years that Schacht was CEO, he will always be remembered and honored for slashing prices 30 percent in the mid 80s to thwart Japanese takeover of America's truck engine market,[14] well before the company could identify, let alone cut, commensurate cost, as well as for constantly maintaining support of R&D by increasing funding sixteen out of those seventeen years. For decades, Cummins spent 5 percent of its revenues on R&D!

Acknowledging Schacht's contribution at a board of directors dinner on July 13, 1992, to mark his thirtieth anniversary with Cummins, Miller said, "The concept of what this company had to become, though constantly changing in detail, has been [Schacht's]. Only now has it become a possibility... there have been many false starts, more disappointments than successes. But, to me—he has been right and I feel a responsibility to say so."[15]

In truth, it appears that Schacht for some time had wanted to move on to bigger and better things. We earlier saw where Schacht and Henderson, with Miller's knowledge and blessing, had hired Mike Walsh in 1984, putting him in a relay race (ostensibly to replace Henderson, who would replace Schacht). But something doesn't add up: bringing in his own replacement seemed like an odd move—Schacht and Henderson were only fifty years old and retirement, say at sixty-five, was a long ways away.

According to John T. Hackett, former vice president of finance and CFO, Schacht, it turns out, was "spending the majority of his time attempting to arrange a merger with a larger company where he and Henderson would emerge as the CEO and COO," thus making way for Walsh to become CEO of Cummins. "There were long discussions with United Technology [*sic*], John Deere, Alcoa and several other larger companies. Of course, nothing ever materialized, which was a blessing, but an immense amount of money was spent with lawyers, investment bankers and consultants pursuing those ideas. [Schacht] really wanted to manage a much larger enterprise. We were using capital at a phenomenal rate. By 1986, [Schacht] and I had established a strong disagreement about the strategic course of CMI. AS CFO, I thought the major merger idea was the wrong direction."[16]

There is nothing in the ISM collection that indicated Miller's view on Cummins being merged with a much larger company. He was not a fan of mergers and acquisitions—even of the "friendly" sort,[17] and certainly not of the "hostile" variety as we discuss regarding the Hanson takeover attempt.

Evidently, Schacht, though, yearned to be set free of Cummins, as he managed to step down as Cummins's CEO on July 12, 1994, at age sixty[18] and ceded the chairmanship six months later in February 1995. His pretext, as he told the *New York Times*, was this: "I felt this company should not face a double retirement and needed a phased succession." And, indeed, it opened the way for Tim Solso to become president and COO under Henderson, who moved into Schacht's position as chairman and CEO.

Will Miller, who joined the board in 1989, says that Cummins's directors were "incredulous" and that to him Schacht's move "seemed really strange."[19]

In our mind, a classic example of turning the other cheek, Miller stood behind his man, stating at Cummins's annual meeting on April 4, 1995, that "Henry Schacht is very probably the ablest CEO of his generation in American business... Henry intuitively understands that great companies are built only steadily and over a long period of time... He has been committed to build Cummins into one of the great companies of the next century. He has won the support of a great board, and he has put together a great team for this effort. He has simultaneously maintained financial strength and achieved technical and manufacturing goals, and... faced down [the Hanson takeover]."[20]

Schacht's real motive became clear when a couple of months later it was announced that he was to become chairman and CEO of Lucent Technologies, the much-larger-than-Cummins manufacturing arm spun out of AT&T.

It must have been hard for Miller to keep the composure of the devout Christian he was. He'd done all sorts of things for Schacht, personally selecting him as his heir apparent years earlier in 1969. He'd protected him through all the tough times. He'd got him on the Yale Corporation and saw him appointed trustee of the Ford Foundation and director of AT&T and sponsored him as a member of the Links club.

Oddly, though he left the Cummins management team, Schacht not only stayed on the board but replaced Miller as chairman of the executive committee. (Miller let Schacht continue to serve on Cummins's board until 1999, six years after his retirement, when, we gather, Solso insisted that he leave.) Jim Henderson, retiring in 2000, wanted to stay on, but Tim Solso refused to let him, evidently.

In 1985, Miller and his wife, Xenia, dedicated the Visitors' Center, as one of their many gifts to Columbus, Indiana.
Provided by The Republic, Columbus, Indiana

14

The Passion Projects Live On

While Miller's leadership at Cummins increasingly took a backseat, he still wielded great influence as a trustee of the Yale Corporation. Miller's efforts with Yale in the 1960s mainly involved helping president Kingman Brewster steer through the tumult of the civil rights revolution to open enrollment to blacks and females, his time in the 1970s centered on philanthropy (his and others).

Inculcated in their upbringing and reinforced by their religion, charitable contribution was central to the lives of Miller and his sister, Clementine Tangeman. Over their lifetimes, they (including Xenia) gave 30 percent of their pretax income each year to charities, which son Will calculates totaled around $120 million for his mother and father, or half of their net worth.[1] On top of this, Cummins Engine from the 1950s on gave 5 percent of its pretax profits to worthy causes.

Never nearly as well endowed as archrival Harvard University, Yale initiated in 1973 a fund drive to raise $370 million. "The 'Campaign for Yale' was the largest campaign undertaken by any university in the world up to that time," Miller would recall.[2] He was one of three cochairman. Lasting six years, the effort commanded an extraordinary amount of his time, and his zeal had to have been tried when his dear friend and protégé Kingman Brewster resigned as Yale's president to become ambassador to Great Britain in 1977.

A year before the drive ended, Miller (ever the dour realist) wrote Brewster's successor, A. Bartlett Giamatti[3]: "We have already determined that, by itself, this sum is inadequate to sustain Yale's quality indefinitely in a future that is characterized by 6% inflation... the annual need, from here on out, is no less than $50,000,000, and after some passage of time this too will have to be increased..."[4]

Five years into the funding efforts trouble erupted. Harold B. Higgins, one of his trusted assistants, advised Miller on December 6, 1978, "The leadership effort has collapsed." Undaunted, Miller personally conducted a challenge fund drive that put the Campaign for Yale over the top, raising $374.3 million by June 30, 1979.[5]

Miller once calculated that "we have, as a family, given Yale more [money] than any other institution"[6] and that their gifts totaled just over $17 million,[7] which amounts to around one-seventh of the charitable contributions in their lifetimes.

What Miller described as the "largest gift we have ever made,"[8] $9.5 million (of the $17 million) was specifically bequeathed to create at Yale the Institute of Sacred Music (or ISM—the same initials as the family's foundation!).

The Institute resulted from the confluence of two factors:

> First was the long-held thought that within the donors' minds that Yale provided a uniquely "right" environment for a school devoted to the training of musicians for the church [and] second was the unhappy decision taken by Union [Theological] Seminary that financial difficulties... dictated [closing] their school of sacred music after forty-five years.[9]

The Institute, moved from New York City to the Yale campus, programmatically would fit between the Divinity School and School of Music, physically would inhabit some of the Divinity School's space, and politically would be "on a par with, and in no way subservient to," the two schools.[10]

Describing the rationale for creating the Institute of Sacred Music at Yale, Clementine wrote then president Brewster (certainly with her brother's approval, likely with his editing):

Our society is in danger of developing a contempt for the minority of poor, and disadvantaged, and helpless. In recalling us to such concern and to the unpalatable truth that we save our lives only by losing them, the compassionate artist has often been the best preacher among us.

In a generation busily plundering and despoiling the planet, Hayden's 'Creation' tells us more eloquently than all the computer runs from all the agencies what our world and our relations with our fellows could be like— if we are able to listen with our hearts as well as with our minds. Mozart's fragment of a 'Requiem' reveals to us a human spirit never at ease on this planet, yet desperately not yet ready to die. The revelation, if perceived, helps us to come to terms with our contradictory selves and our situation.

And the understanding of our own endless capacity to attack and kill that small best part of our own selves, the God within us, comes home to us, as nowhere else, in the final chorus of the St. Matthew's Passion...

We hope that, in this new institution, the function of music and the arts in Christianity will receive new strength through the preparation and training of individual musicians, artists and teachers who understand their calling in broad Christian terms...[11]

Construction of the Institute of Sacred Music was started in November 1975, while Brewster was still Yale's president. Evidently, Miller and his sister were pleased with its development. Attending a creative festival in 1979, Miller noted it "embodied everything we had hoped the Institute might someday become."[12] There was a brief flare-up between Miller and Giamatti in 1981 when the administration decided to deny tenure to the ISM Director as was given the deans of the Divinity School and School of Music—Miller calling it "a raw power play" and saying, "We've both been had."[13] This dispute, however, got resolved to Miller's satisfaction.

While Yale received a great deal from Miller, Miller got a lot from Yale. First were deep friendships, especially with the other trustees (a most unusual group of men), in particularly Brewster, president of Yale during unquestionably the most turbulent time in its long history—before or since.

While mentoring Brewster, however, it needs to be underscored that Miller was learning from Brewster. "[To] assertions from some alumni that 'Brewster must go,'" Miller responded,

> As a manager myself, I am perhaps more than normally aware of the limits to the powers of any job. The manager's crystal ball is forever clouded as he tries to discern the future's shape. Hindsight for us critics is, however, always 20/20. The manager works through others, and seldom directly. He must gain a high level of consensus, or nothing can happen. Compromise, acquiescence, and delay are part of his job.[14]

Certainly relevant words of advice for Miller himself, as he and Cummins Engine embarked on the most difficult two decades in the company's history.

Finally, Miller received an honorary degree from his alma mater in May 1979. "Nothing has meant or will mean as much to me," he wrote Sam Chauncey.[15]

In Chauncey's view, nobody did as much for Yale in the twentieth century as Miller.[16] But there is nothing to commemorate his contribution—no plaque on a building, no statue on a mall, no name on a professorship—exactly the way Miller wanted.

Miller was now seventy years old, and yet he found the energy and resolve to build yet another church—the fourth to be born of the faith and generosity of the Irwin-Sweeney-Miller family. Sweeney Chapel at Christian Theological Seminary, or CTS (Indianapolis), was completed in 1987.

Ironically, Miller had for a time distanced himself from CTS. We earlier saw how Miller had been so heavily involved in his great-uncle's "other legacy," the Disciples' Seminary, prying it loose from Butler, setting up its own campus, and serving as its chairman (1958–1965) when his term, per the bylaws, ended. Miller's "leadership had been constructive and exacting... his commitment to excellence and... managerial style... never seemed to release the pressure to perform."[17]

As narrated, Richard B. Stoner, then second in command at Cummins, succeeded Miller as chairman at CTS and served a three-year term but evidently did not near match his predecessor's performance (that, particularly, may have been a key factor in Miller's decision in 1969 to choose Schacht, not Stoner, as his successor at the engine company).

Without Miller as chairman, the seminary drifted. On January 11, 1968, George Newlin, head of Irwin Management, wrote his boss an alarming memo: "CTS—what now?" With $1.6 million of debt, Newlin declared that the school was "drifting and aimless... The President is the problem." Newlin was referring to Bradford A. Norris, whose term had begun in 1959, concurrent with Miller's stepping down. Newlin continued, "I think it would be difficult, if not impossible, for us to offer sideline leadership and guidance to a school for which [it now seems clear] you provide the leadership... I see CTS as the bottom of the list of [your] very demanding priorities—Cummins, Presidential Commissions, Yale, Ford, Church."

Miller initially reacted a bit defensively. He rejoined (in red ink at the bottom of Newlin's note), "What added plant is needed? Very little. How good faculty and students really are? Not bad."[18]

A week later, though, Miller sent (though not specified as such) a "terminal check" for $1.6 million to wipe out CTS debt, bringing the family's contribution to the school to "more than $11 million," and Miller and his sister, Clementine, then both resigned from the board.[19]

Norris would continue to head the seminary until early 1974, and there is no evidence of communication between him and Miller. However, "hardly had Norris' successor [Thomas J. Liggett] taken over as President [that February] he was visited by Miller and Stoner [still an active board member]."[20] (The US economy was bedeviled by recession and inflation at the time.)

"Miller asked the President what he was going to do to face the crisis," and he ticked off steps like reducing the draw on CTS's endowment, cutting costs, freezing salaries, and increasing fund-raising efforts.

After listening to the report, Miller "looked at Stoner and announced they may as well go back to Columbus. 'The Seminary's going to make it.'"[21]

And indeed it did. In the thirteen years of his presidency (1974–1987), Liggett lifted CTS's endowment from $2.7 million to $36 million, enrollment and curricula doing well too. Miller wrote Liggett shortly before his retirement, "The Disciples owe you a debt of gratitude as their real leader in a time when great leadership in Protestant Christianity is almost non-existent."[22] "A year later Miller asserted that [Liggett] literally "saved the Seminary" from extinction, maintained it as a vital force in the denomination... and restored the endowment to a size I would never have guessed possible."[23]

Among other positives, Liggett's leadership emboldened Miller's family to underwrite the design and construction of the last missing piece on the CTS campus—a chapel, costing $6 million and paid for by Clementine Tangeman.[24] In our view, there is no way Miller's family could have made the contribution without the enterprise resting on secure financial footings.

Edward Larrabee Barnes, who'd done the CTS campus to date, got the commission to design the church in a pre-Gothic style.

In a playful letter to T. J., Miller weighed in with his thoughts on what to call the structure. He admitted,

I do not feel that naming the Chapel should be the prerogative of the donors. The Trustees... should decide this... I am expressing my views to you because you asked for them.

I confess that in these dehumanized times I wave a flag for human names. I think that Yale University and Harvard University are more friendlier names than Massachusetts Institute of Technology or East Texas A and M... I also like what Columbus has done in naming its elementary schools for beloved teachers. Lillian Schmitt School is better to me than Elementary School #304... I find myself mildly saddened by such names as "First United Methodist Church" and "Country Club Christian Church." We are surrounded by a cloud of witnesses, and we should hold before ourselves the worthy labors of those who preceded us, from whose examples we can take inspiration.

Why "Sweeney Chapel"...? ... Z. T. Sweeney was not a fat cat giver. He was an effective and memorable minister of the gospel, whose idea has now after so many years resulted in today's CTS... Here endeth my disjointed thoughts... The decision is yours.[25]

And Reverend Liggett chose Sweeney Chapel as the name of the new church, which Miller would write "seems to me to be a splendid building."[26]

As inscription on the memorial plaque for the chapel, Miller and his family chose from 2 Peter 1:5–8:

Make every effort to supplement your faith with virtue and virtue with knowledge and knowledge with self control and self control with steadfastness and steadfastness with Godliness and Godliness with brotherly affection and brotherly affection with love. For if these things are yours and abound, they keep you from being ineffective or unfruitful in the knowledge of our Lord Jesus Christ.[27]

Marilyn Keiser, head of the Organ Department of the School of Music at Indiana University, played at the opening event on November 5, 1987, dedicating the Holtkamp organ. Though she recalls there were issues with acoustics of the spoken word ("The preachery struggled"), "it produced almost glorious sound—it needed a reverberant environment. It's a beautiful organ," she told the author. "I loved it."[28]

"With the dedication of the new Sweeney Chapel, the material form of [CTS] was finally complete and its program of theological studies had reached full maturity... many would have said that the objective of [Reverend] Liggett... had been achieved—that CTS had become 'the finest institution of its kind ever developed by the Disciples.'"[29]

Miller could take satisfaction knowing he completed "the cathedral", whose foundation was laid down decades ago by his ancestors, most notably his grandmother, Linnie Sweeney, and his great uncle W. G. Irwin.

15

One Last Fight

Christmas of 1988 was ruined when, on December 23, Miller found out that British conglomerate Hanson PLC declared it had bought nearly 10 percent of Cummins's common stock.[1] Hanson had a history of gaining control of troubled industrial businesses and dismembering them—Cummins was officially "in play."[2] At age seventy-nine, Miller was about to enter into one of the greatest battles of his life in business.

Brooke Tuttle, longtime Cummins executive who'd become director of economic development for Columbus's chamber of commerce, observed, "I don't think the people of Columbus really comprehended what would happen if Hanson had gotten hold of Cummins. Hanson would have split it up, spun off parts of the company. It would have been a shell of its former self."[3]

The engine company, frankly, was a fiscal mess at this point. It had lost money in three of the last four years. Its balance sheet at the end of 1988 listed eleven types of long-term debt, plus a convertible preferred stock, and the annual report would disclose that the company was routinely selling ("factoring" is the formal word) "up to $100 million" of its accounts receivables at a time, for which services Cummins had paid $8.3 million in 1988.

"We outside Board members were pessimistic about being able to survive [Hanson's] attack," Don Perkins, the director, told the author. "The Board didn't know what to do until Will [Miller] came along."[4] Will's idea, as explained in *The Engine That Could*, involved his family making two "sacrifices": first, his father, mother, and aunt, using mostly

142

borrowed funds to buy Hanson's common shares for $72 million, which was $5 million over the market price; then, second, to exchange the common for convertible notes that quickly morphed into convertible preferred shares (to help Cummins's balance sheet) but waiving a 6 percent premium to help the company.[5]

But two much more important aspects of the buyout are not adequately examined in *The Engine That Could*, which apparently got a close editing from Miller,[6] always so modest. First, the Miller family was taking a huge risk, in our opinion. Cummins at this point easily could have been forced to file for Chapter XI bankruptcy protection— there was so little margin for error given its highly leveraged balance sheet. In such event, the family might have lost close to 60 percent of its net worth (see table below). The engine company was sliding downhill, (with losses per share of $0.19 in 1989, $1.81 in 1990, and $0.62 in 1991 and warranty expenses that went from 1.9 percent of sales in 1987, to 2.9 percent in 1988, and 4.0 percent in 1989, due to the horrible launch of the NT88 engine.

Miller Family Balance Sheet*
6/30/1990
($Millions)

	As Presented to Counsel	Pro Forma if Cummins Went Bankrupt
Assets		
"Liquid" Assets	44.7	44.7
Cummins (Preferred) [(1)]	104.7	0
Irwin Union Bank Stock	7.2	7.2
Tipton Lakes Co.	8.4	8.4
"Personal Assets"	57.8	6.3 [(2)]
Other	9.1	9.1
Total Assets	231.9	75.7

Liabilities

Chemical Bank Loan	51.5	0	
Charitable Pledges	(1.2)	(1.2)	
Total Liabilities	52.7	1.2	
Net Worth	$179.2	$74.5	-58.5%

- Consisting of Clementine Tangeman, Xenia Miller, and Irwin Miller

    (1) Family now owns about 15 percent of stock, up from 5 percent (but down from the sixty five percent it owned in 1959); net of Chemical Bank loan, Cummins stock equals $53.2 million net worth, or 29.7 percent of total

    (2) Assumes sufficient liquidity to pay off Chemical Bank loan

As shown in this pro forma family balance sheet, buying Hanson's 10 percent interest in Cummins, added to their 5 percent, meant Miller was risking nearly 60 percent of his family's net worth to save the engine company. And this would be before their natural instinct kicked in to provide charity to Cummins employees potentially thrown out of work around the world.

Additionally, assuming the deal got done with Hanson, neither Miller nor his sister might be alive to see the results. In a memo to the Office Committee Union dated June 6, 1993, Miller recounted,

> My family and I incurred a substantial cash loss several years ago to help prevent a hostile takeover by a firm, who would have [we thought] slowly liquidated the Company, leaving no long-term for anybody.

> That long-term future will probably not be fully realized in my lifetime (I am 84; my sister is 88). But I am excited about its possibility and the jobs it will create, whether I am around or not.[8]

It was as if Miller willed Cummins Engine, for now, to exist and, ultimately, to excel. On October 2, 1994, in a speech to the combined members of North Christian Church and Saint Paul's Episcopal Church in Columbus, Miller picked up the theme again, albeit in a religious context: "Instead of knowledge, I have faith, a faith I hope I would live and die for, not a faith always held in the full realization that is not knowledge. It is not total truth and cannot ever be in this life. We should listen for new truth, and always be receptive to it, but we are not to forget the words of Paul: 'We walk by faith and not by sight.'"[9]

Miller was, indeed, like those "cathedral builders of the 12th century, who were content to make great plans and to lay in their lifetimes no more than footings and foundations, if this is all they could get done— never seeing the end result."[10]

While hoping to give Schacht more time to find new investors, Miller must have been deeply concerned about the company that he'd salvaged from Hanson, effective July 17, 1989. Cummins's main market was in a recession—industry orders for heavy-duty trucks fell 42 percent from first quarter of 1989 to first quarter of 1990.[11] Cummins's share— due to the botched launch of the NT88 and the amazing debut of Detroit Diesel's Series 60—would drop almost steadily from 50 percent in 1989, to 46 percent in 1990, to 38 percent in1991, and to 35 percent in 1992.

The company was in clear financial distress: as at December 31, 1989 its balance sheet showed a current ratio (assets versus liabilities) of just 1.3 and a debt/equity ratio of merely 0.7.[12] Cummins's avenues to borrowing more money blocked by a highly leveraged balance sheet, Schacht's sole recourse was selling equity, but that didn't work, either. As example, Cummins's longtime Japanese partner yet competitor, Komatsu Ltd., refused Schacht's offer to sell them 15 percent of Cummins in October 1989.[13]

Yet Miller's buyout of Hanson won Cummins time—time to get control of the quality issues vexing its product. Finally, on July 16, 1990 (a day short of one year since Miller's purchase), Cummins announced agreement to sell four million shares of its stock for $250 million to

Ford Motor Company, Tenneco Inc., and Kubota Ltd., with a six-year "standstill" agreement not to sell. Simultaneously, Cummins announced it was using the bulk of these proceeds to reduce its long-term debt to "just over $300 million" (down from $473 million in the previous year)—a huge accomplishment for management, mainly Schacht.

In fact, things were looking somewhat brighter for the engine company. In a memo to Miller date September 25, 1990, F. Joseph Loughery, vice president of heavy-duty engines (and later president under Solso), wrote,

> Our 1991 engines are being well received by customers [who perceive them] better than the competitors' in performance, durability, and fuel economy and as a result we can regain lost market share... our technical work to meet emissions [requirements], while improving performance and fuel economy has caught the attention of our industry. This is the single biggest reason why Tennaco [*sic*], Ford and Kubota invested $250,000,000 in Cummins and why the downturn doesn't overly concern them.[14]

In our view, though, Cummins never could have attracted these corporate investors if Miller had not bought out Hanson—it was his grandest deed!

Sometime in the frightening times of the late 1980s, Miller made an impromptu call on Schacht and Henderson at corporate headquarters and told them in no uncertain terms that he would not let them sell the engine part of Cummins and to stop trying.[15] He then put his money where his mouth was by buying out Hanson, as we've seen. Miller was absolutely unwavering in his commitment to building the world's best diesels, far into the future, long after he was gone.

At first, it seemed as if his wager on Cummins was a bad bet. The company would lose a record $138 million in 1990 (largely due to the bungled launch of the NT88).[16]

That November, still chairman of the executive committee, he and his directors received a six-page, single-spaced, typewritten letter from an anonymous employee:

> We are running out of time... to restore the company to the status it once held in the industry... current management has lost the confidence of employees at all levels ... and are viewed as 'out of touch' and lacking in the areas of leadership and direction. They were not appointed based on accomplishments. Schacht gained his position as President at the age of 34, having worked at Irwin Management, his background in finance. Henderson, appointed President with a background in personnel, an area as poorly managed as the operations of the company... We at Cummins urge you to take necessary steps to remove Schacht and Henderson, replacing them with executives who understand the business of manufacturing, people, and the markets we serve.

Obviously unable to respond directly to his unnamed critic, Miller, with his felt pen, jotted down his thoughts for the file.

> The writer is correct in some matters—but writer is highly selective—omits the big accomplishments.

> Prior to 1980: CECo = one-engine company = NT... [1] Decision made by Board (long-term) this position was dangerously unstable.... [2] Co. brought out successfully 10L... and met target goals. Neither CAT (Caterpillar)/ DDA (Detroit Diesel Allison)—10 yrs. later... have

done this.... [3] Co. brought out B/C engines 6L/8L successfully... (neither) CAT/DDA.... [4] Met cost and quality objectives.... [5] Co. Committe [*sic*] $1 billion + to this.... [6] CECo = only U.S. Mfr with 6, 8, 10, 14L line – in production, good quality, emissions qual[ified] and tested thru 1991. What happened? The Japanese... We can be criticized 4 having met their prices B/4 we [met their] costs but no Japanese diesels made or sold in USA. [Long] term I still think = right decision, This Bd. debated it at length—approved decision... CECo '91 products = very good... CAT in disarray... DDA has only 1 engine.[17]

On July 13, 1992, at a board of directors dinner celebrating Schacht's thirtieth anniversary with the company, Miller, now eighty-three, praised his team for dealing with

obstacles that no company should have to face... attempts at hostile takeovers... a prolonged recession... furious discounting of the Company's main money maker [while] our research and development expenses had to be more than tripled... rushing into production the '88 engines before they were ready... It is no wonder so many—inside and outside the company—said "Cummins is a goner"... The job of remaking the Company, of course, isn't over—but our performance in the [last 18 months] is giving most of the naysayers... the opportunity to re-discover Cummins, as the successful example of what every company ought to have done during all those years in which they had said "sell the stock"... Our share... has turned around... There is good evidence we have the best products... the [B and C] engines are not only the best world-wide, but are profitable and have a solid decade of growth ahead... our costs are down… our quality, never good enough, has reached levels which surprise me… the light at the end of the tunnel is not that of some speeding locomotive of doom, but instead a most exciting and very bright complex of opportunities which all of you—through very frightening times—have yourselves constructed.

So Henry, as the fellow said who jumped off the roof as he passed the 10th floor, "so far, so good." Only I would add, the house was on fire; it was right to jump, and there's a strong net down there, which you had the biggest hand in making.

And Miller presented Schacht with the pin Don Tull had given him twenty-five years earlier.[18] Sadly, although the loss in 1991 had been trimmed to just $14 million, Cummins produced a deficit of $190 million in 1992, the largest in its history.

In April 1994, Miller stepped down as chairman of the executive committee and was replaced by Schacht, although (as seen) he'd resigned as Cummins's chairman and within months became CEO and chairman of Lucent Technologies.

Never inattentive to the engine company, however, Miller that summer handwrote a note to Tim Solso (now president, having replaced Henderson, who'd become CEO and chairman): "In times of good earnings in past years Cummins has usually lost control of hiring. Everyone adds people. Quality of new hires declines. Is this happening today? In past 12 months, we have added 257 exempts. Are they all outstanding? Are they all needed?—Please do not bother to reply to me (I mean it)… Final question: When the next downturn comes, will we have another massive layoff of the very people we are now so rapidly hiring?"[19] Even at age 85, he couldn't let go!

With the new team of Henderson and Solso at the top, Cummins's profits hit a record high of $253 million in 1994. Yet, unfortunately, another bungled start-up lay in wait.

In a December 1996 letter, also to Solso, in regard the pending Apex engine, Miller rather playfully asks, "What are we going to name this engine? 'Apex' implies that this is as far as we know how to go."[20] Also known as Signature 600, this was a fifteen-liter motor designed to meet EPA's 2004 emission standards and also to replace the venerable NH. Miller, who would resign from the board the next year (1997), as usual, was prescient.

Cummins spent $1 billion on the Apex project, or as much as it had on the B and C launches in the 1980s. "We bet our company a second time," said Henderson.[21] Sadly, Apex was to become "the worst engine launch ever," in the words of Robert J. ("Bob") Weimer, Cummins's vice president of quality (and thus in a position to know).[22]

In no small way, thanks to Apex (which morphed into ISX 15), Cummins's bottom-line performance was lackluster the next few years, and profits would not reach a new peak ($350 million) until 2004, the year of Miller's death at age ninety-five.

What a shame Miller was not alive to see the results established by Solso and his team! During Solso's tenure, Cummins's profits would soar (with but one year's interruption) to $1.8 billion in 2011. While reflective of R&D achievements of past decades, Solso's success in large measure stemmed from bold new initiatives (e.g., cancelling an engine program, ending customer discounting, buying out distributors, and outsourcing manufacturing) and tough-minded management. Just what Miller had hoped!

16

Saying Good-Bye

Conrad Bowling, president of the Diesel Workers Union, used the occasion of Cummins's 1997 annual shareholders' meeting to make Miller an honorary lifetime member, saying, "This is perhaps unprecedented in the world of labor relations, but you are unprecedented in the world of business leadership... You were at the top of the company with lots of strategic world issues vying for your attention, yet you always had time for those of us on the shop floor dealing with the issues of today's production. We could talk to you and we knew you would listen. You came to our gatherings, and we know that you cared."[1]

Miller would lead a mostly private life after this, with one notable exception: his very public support in March 2000 of Solso's decision that Cummins would provide "traditional benefits... to employees' life partners who are not legal spouses." Miller wrote a widely circulated letter to Solso: "I understand the need to find the very best people to work for Cummins. The best talent has never come from one segment of the population, whether defined by race, gender or other aspects of a person's background... Judgment is not for us to pass but God."[2]

Advancing age was causing problems. In April 1994, he'd got a new shoulder "for an old arthritic one,"[3] and that July (he was eighty-five and Xenia seventy-nine), he wrote Kevin Roche a charming note that "neither we (at our advanced ages) nor our friends feel safe in going down to the pit, nor in exiting there from, so we don't use it. What can you do?"[4] The "pit," of course, was the sunken conversational area in the living room of their home at 2760 Highland Way—Kevin, of course, working for Eero Saarinen when he designed the house (the solution was to install a brass banister and provide thicker seat cushions—not as far to sit down or get up!), according to Carolyn McKin Spicer, the Millers' housekeeper from 1989 to 2008, when Xenia died.[5]

Through the late nineties, Miller occasionally went to his office at 301 Washington to which now he was usually driven. (He liked to loop around the south of the city and come into Columbus across the new suspension bridge.) More and more, though, he would have his mail sent home and work out of the former gardener's shed that Alexander Girard had redesigned.

The Millers continued to spend about five months of the year away from Columbus—January through March in Hobe Sound and July and August in Canada. Miller, however, had a mini-stroke (the first of several) in mid-2000,[6] and the following spring he sold their Florida home which "would not hold ourselves, the professional help we now require and family guests."[7]

The staff at 2760 Highland Way through the nineties consisted of Carolyn McKin Spicer, housekeeper, and her husband, Wayne, groundskeeper, who lived next door. Carolyn typically fixed the Millers' breakfast and lunch, and Claire Gregory most times made supper (the diet consistently healthy). Starting in 2000, though, due to his failing health, Miller employed a team of caretakers, who took turns serving Miller as needed around the clock, one being Benjamin L. ("Ben") Wever.

In 2002, Xenia was afflicted with dementia that grew steadily worse.[8] Ben says, though, Miller "was so in love with Xenia until the end… he didn't want to be taken to a nursing home, as he felt it was important to be there for Xenia."[9]

Wever and Spicer separately stated that Miller was mentally sharp until the end of his life. Wever says that "nobody was as kind or generous" as his boss. "He'd say 'thank you, sir' to a twenty-three-year old!" Spicer recalled Miller being "the most kind, compassionate person you'd ever met." Wever added, "You could feel the greatness when you were around him. Everyone [on the staff] would give him their all."

The summer of 2004, Miller's health deteriorated such that he was brought back to Columbus from Muskoka. His five children ("M5," he'd dubbed them) were called to come to Columbus given the gravity of their father's condition. They had gone outside for a moment, leaving Wever alone in the bedroom with their dad when Wever said Miller sat up, took one last breath, and died in his arms.[10]

Miller had planned his funeral in detail well in advance. A four-page letter to his son Will in 1998 described the arrangements, with instructions including the following:

> The burial service should be in the morning. Only family mourners and pallbearers should attend... the memorial service should be in the afternoon at NCC [North Christian Church] and open to all who wish to attend... undertaker personnel should be invisible...

> The one thing I am adamant on is that my memorial service should include the music of J. S. Bach... At the start of the service, use the same chorale prelude that Bach chose for his own funeral service... "Before Thy Throne I Stand"... Do not play hymns too fast... The conclusion should be the St. Anne Fugue of Bach played at full strength and stately pace (include a note asking the congregation to remain seated until the Fugue is completed).[11]

And so, on August 16th, 2004, ended the story of "one of the great, great men of our times" (the words of Henry Schacht).[12]

Miller could join his ancestors in the next life, satisfied like them, he'd given his all in performing good works, some unfinished, awaiting completion by the next generation.

Acknowledgments

I want to acknowledge Sheila Behrman, who typed this manuscript, Will Cockrell, who supervised the editing process, and Hari Chelluri, who compiled the Cummins financial data.

Endnotes

Prologue

[1] James A. Henderson, interview with the author, February 23, 2012.

[2] Irwin-Sweeney-Miller (ISM) collection, Indiana Historical Society, box 542, folder 4, Columbus.

[3] Henderson, interview, February 23, 2012.

[4] Tom Bonnell, interview with the author, June 19, 2013; "The architect wanted to plant wild flowers and prairie grass around the facility, but JIM objected."

[5] Alexander Girard, letter, November 25, 1965, box 359, folder 6; "A. Black and white only—no additional colors; B. Printed or offset—no engraving; C. Capable of looking well when done by a local printer on normal business paper."

[6] Henderson, interview, February 23, 2012.

[7] Henry B. Schacht, interview by David Bollier, 1992.

[8] Ed Booth, interview with the author, March 22, 2013.

[9] Susan Hanafee, interview with the author, May 17, 2012.

[10] Caroyln McKin Spicer, interview with the author, February 14, 2013.

[11] John Bean, interview with the author, March 16, 2012.

[12] Irwin Miller, remarks, Pritzker Exhibit preview, Indianapolis Museum of Art, May 20, 1993, box 545, folder 21.

[13] Box 479, folder 5, June 11 1993.

Chapter 1

[1] Per Harry McCawley, former associate editor, *The Republic*; the courthouse remained Columbus's tallest structure until erection of First Christian Church, topping out at 162 feet in 1942.

[2] Jon Dilts, *The Magnificent 92 Indiana Court Houses* (Bloomington, IN: Rose Bud Press, 1991).

[3] Irwin Miller, interview with Robert Stewart, November 13, 1995.

[4] J . L. Cruikshank and D. B. Sicilia, *The Engine That Could* (Watertown, MA: Harvard Business School Press, 1997), 18.

[5] With railroad construction in Indiana essentially complete by this time, Columbus had not been targeted by east-west rail probably because of the forbiddingly deep valleys in counties to the East (which parenthetically diverted ox-drawn wagons of German and Eastern European immigrants to the north or south of Columbus).

[6] Irwin Miller, interview with Robert Stewart, November 13, 1995.

[7] T. George Harris, "Egghead in the Diesel Industry," *Fortune* (October 1957).

[8] H.T. Miller, lectures, 1983, 19, box 540, folder 5.

[9] Indiana's two incumbent US senators.

[10] *Columbus (IN) Evening Republican*, April 19, 1909, 1.

[11] *Columbus (IN) Evening Republican*, April 24, 1909, 1.

[12] Ibid.

[13] Cruikshank, 28.

[14] Lyle Cummins, *The Diesel Odyssey of Clessie Cummins* (Wilsonville, OR: Carnot Press, 1998), 25.

[15] Cruikshank, 28.

[16] Cruikshank.

[17] William I. Miller, interview with the author, September 9, 2013.

[18] Ibid.

[19] Irwin Miller, interview, November 13, 1995.

[20] C. L. Cummins, *My Days with the Diesel* (Philadelphia, PA, Chilton Co.,1967), 112.

[21] Box 39, folder 4; "To M5," July 7, 1993.

[22] Box 542, folder 4; written in 1995 at Muskoka.

[23] H. T. Miller, lectures, 1983, box 540, folder 15.

[24] Yale Divinity School, address, box 173, folder 1.

[25] ISM, box 540, folder 15, 13.

[26] William Miller, interview with the author, September 18, 2013.

[27] Irwin Miller, letter to Arthur J. Ungerleder, March 15, 1976, box 468, folder 8.

[28] Yale Divinity School, speech, September 4, 1985, box 452, folder 1.

[29] Pettigrew Seminar, April 27, 1998, box 545, folder 37.

[30] L. Cummins, 268; Clessie L. Cummins, letter to Irwin Miller et al., 1939.

[31] Ibid, 270-271.

[32] Irwin Miller, interview, November 13, 1995.

[33] Ibid.

[34] Ibid.

[35] Ibid.

[36] Ibid.

[37] Box 25, folder 6, January 23, 1967, 3–4.

[38] Cruikshank, 61.

[39] Cruikshank, 141, 159.

Chapter 2

[1] Lynchburg College, speech, 1985, box 281, folder 6.

[2] Dorothy Kalin, *Town and Country*, July 1974.

[3] Guild Press of indiana

[4] Watkins, pg. 5

[5] Watkins, pg 16

[6] Watkins, pg 28

[7] Watkins, pg 27

[8] Watkins, pg 30

[9] Watkins, pg 32

[10] Watkins, pgs 35-37

[11] Watkins, pgs 44-45

[12] Watkins, pgs, 57-58

[13] Watkins, pg 67

[14] William I. Miller interview, September 9, 2013

[15] Watkins, pg. 77

16   Watkins, pgs 87-89

17   Watkins, pg 9

18   Watkins, pg 91

19   Harris, 128

20   Personal biography, December 31, 1986, box 542, folder 4.

21   C. Cummins, 65.

22   Box 544, folder 3.

23   Box 544, folder 3.

24   Harris, 129.

25   Irwin Miller, letter to Stephen Wenkey, September 13, 1983, box 422, folder 3.

26   Harris, 129.

27   William Miller, interview, September 18, 2013.

28   Ibid.

29   Box 93, folder 7.

30   Ibid. Interestingly, Miller's best marks came in math: Greek, 85 percent; Latin, 80 percent, English, 88 percent; trigonometry, 94 percent; and solid geometry, 98 percent.

31   ISM (DMB 135), box 3.

Chapter 3

1   Box 205, folder 2.

2   Cruikshank, 10.

3   As a contrast, when he served years later on the Yale Corporation (equivalent of a board of directors), everyone else (all alumni, of course) except president Kingman Brewster and he had belonged to a secret society (and Brewster had been tapped but declined); J. Irwin Miller, interview by Geoff Kabaservice, December 10, 1991; Grisword/Brewster history project.

4   Box 280, folder 3.

5   Box 460, folder 1.

6   William I. Miller, interview with the author, April 13, 2012.

7   Harris, 282.

[8] Box 496, folder 7; besides, when finally Miller visited Union Starch, he found that "the plant had been run down. It was unbelievably filthy… costs were unknown, labor relations were terrible. We even had a *foremen's* union, and management was poor and maybe corrupt."

[9] Irwin Miller, interview, November 13, 1995.

[10] L. Cummins, 165.

[11] L. Cummins, 227.

[12] Cruikshank,88.

[13] Cruikshank, 89.

[14] Ibid.

[15] Cruikshank,91.

[16] William I. Miller, interview, September 19, 2013.

[17] L. Cummins, 207.

[18] Cruikshank, 110.

[19] L. Cummins, 229.

[20] L. Cummins, 268–269.

[21] L. Cummins, 231, 233; Miller had a hand in convincing General Electric to take over the project to build the "switch" engines.

[22] L. Cummins, 265.

[23] L. Cummins, 238.

[24] Cruikshank, 103.

[25] Cruikshank, 96.

[26] L. Cummins, 233.

[27] Cruikshank, 195; Tull would become Cummins's fourth president (1960)

[28] Cruikshank, 110.

[29] Cruikshank, 104.

[30] Cruikshank, 105.

[31] Cruikshank, 106.

[32] Cruikshank, 108; the DWU and its clerical worker counterpart, the Office Committee Union (OCU), represent Cummins's Columbus area workers today.

[33] L. Cummins, 65.

Chapter 4

[1] Box 585, folder 9.

[2] Ibid.; they lived at 534 Wilson Street (now Reeves Street) or about where the office of the Diesel Workers Union now sits.

[3] Ibid.

[4] L. Cummins, 295.

[5] Box 487, folder 5; Xenia would be elected chairman of the OCU, 1/43, box 559, folder 1.

[6] Box 464, folder 1.

[7] Box 463, folder 2.

[8] Box 558, folder 11.

[9] Box 463, folder 5.

[10] Box 463, folder 2.

[11] Box 559, folder 1.

[12] Clessie Cummins frequently was in Washington during the war because of his duties on the War Production Board.

[13] L. Cummins, 296.

[14] Box 463, folder 2.

[15] William Miller, interview, April 13, 2013.

[16] Box 464, folder 4.

[17] Box 466, folder 1, *SEAPOWER* (August 1946).

[18] Box 464, folder 8, December 10, 1943.

[19] William Miller, interview, April 13, 2012.

[20] William Miller, interview with author, October 5, 2012.

[21] Box 465, folder 3, February 16, 1944.

[22] Box 464, folder 7, November 5, 1943.

[23] Box 464, folder 8, December 15, 1943.

[24] Box 559, folder 6.

[25] Cruikshank, 124.

[26] Box 464, folder 8, December 13, 1943.

[27] Box 464, folder 9.

[28] Box 465, folder 1.

[29] Box 464, folder 8, December 19, 1943.

[30] Box 465, folder 1, January 4, 1944.

[31] Box 465, folder 1.

[32] Box 466.

[33] Bureau of Naval Personnel, letter to Irwin Miller, October 20, 1946, authorizing him to wear a Navy Unit Commendation Ribbon, box 466, folder 1.

[34] Box 465, folder 9.

[35] Box 488, folder 1.

[36] Box 465, folder 10.

[37] Box 465, folder 1.

[38] Cruikshank, 135.

Chapter 5

[1] Box 488, folder 1.

[2] Ibid.

[3] Cruikshank, 329; a Cummins research engineer said that the PT fuel pump "gave us a minimum of twenty years ahead of everyone else in the market."

[4] Box 25, folder 6, November 3, 1964, 3–4.

[5] Cruikshank, 48.

[6] L. Cummins, 289.

[7] Cruikshank, 124.

[8] Box 465, folder 1, January 9, 1944.

[9] Box 466, folder 1.

[10] Box 24, folder 7.

[11] Cruikshank, 138–139.

[12] Box 25, folder 7.

[13] Cruikshank, 153.

[14] Box 25, folder 8.

[15] Cruikshank, 153.

[16] Cruikshank, 122.

[17] Cruikshank, 123; Henderson, interview, February 23, 2012; Jim Henderson told the author that Miller "loved the book… It told the story."

Chapter 6

1   Yale Divinity School, address, September 4, 1985, box 173, folder 1.

2   John Bean, interview, March 16, 2012. (In a letter, 3/29/00, to Tim M. Solso, chairman of Cummins, on the companies new "domestic partner's policy", Miller wrote that he had read and studied six different passages in the bible pertaining to gays and lesbians; box 463, folder 1)

3   Irwin Miller, "The Theological Basis for Social Action," speech, Convention of Christian Churches (Disciples of Christ), October 19, 1958, box 386, folder 3.

4   James W. Hoffman, "J. Irwin Miller, Churchman and Industrialist," *Presbyterian Life* (February 15, 1962), box 320, folder 2.

5   Irwin Miller, "Freedoms in Tension," *Christian Century* (October 28, 1964).

6   Irwin Miller, "A New Role for Business," speech, University of Chicago, 1967, box 530, folder 3.

7   Irwin Miller, letter to Christopher M. Drew, March 31, 1972, box 215, folder 2.

8   Irwin Miller, "The Christian Life Commission," speech, the Southern Baptist Convention, March 22, 1976, box 537, folder 6.

9   H. T. Miller, "A Pilgrim's Progress," lecture, Christian Theological Seminary, March 16, 1983, box 540, folder 16.

10   Irwin Miller, remarks, Planning Conference, July 27, 1987.

11   "A Celebration of Christian Unity," speech, North Christian Church and Saint Paul's Episcopalian Church, October 2, 1994, box 545, folder 22.

12   Fortieth anniversary, North Christian Church, October 8, 1995, box 545, folder 30.

13   Taft School Commencement, May 31, 1997, box 481, folder 6.

14   101 Pettigrew Faith-in-Action seminar, April 27, 1998, box 545, folder 37.

15   William Miller, interview, October 5, 2012.

16   Box 478, folder 6.

17   William Miller, interview, October 5, 2012.

18   Doug Eckhart, interview with the author, December 18, 2012.

19   Charles H. Webb Jr., interview with the author, December 4, 2012.

20   Irwin Miller, letter to John Nelson, June 24, 1981, box 472, folder 9.

21   William Miller, interview, October 5, 2012.

22 Irwin Miller, letter to Martin E. Marty, January 16, 1989, box 285, folder 3.

23 John Eliot Gardiner, *Bach: Music in the Castle of Heaven* (New York: Alfred A. Knopf, 2013), 129.

24 Irwin Miller, letter to Thomas J. Liggett, April 28, 1982, box 473, folder 5.

Chapter 7

1   Box 443, folder 8.

2   William Miller, interview, April 13, 2012.

3   Michael Sorkin, "Tastemakers—J. Irwin Miller," *House and Garden* (June 1983).

4   Irwin Miller, letter to Kevin Roche, April 16, 1993, box 354, folder 7.

5   Dorothy Kalin, Town & Country, July 1974.

6   Ibid.

7   Principal reasons were role of women and type of Baptism, cited in Chapter XIII.

8   Keith Watkins, *Christian Theological Seminary, Indianapolis* (Zionsville, IN: Guild Press of Indiana, 2001); William Miller, interview, March 18, 2014.

9   Bean, interview.

10 See chapter 6, "The Man and His Passions"

11 Irwin Miller, letter to Reverend Daniel Kechel, December 22, 1964, box 359, folder 6.

12 Presumably with great chagrin, Miller, now chairman of Christian Theological Seminary, decided in the fall of 1960 to exclude Saarinen as a candidate to design a new campus; Watkins, 147.

13 Box 393, folder 1.

14 Ibid.

15 Bean, interview.

16 Box 387, folder 8.

17 Irwin Miller, brochure on Harry Weese, March 1987, box 423 folder 3.

18 Harry Weese, letter to Miller, December 18, 1963, box 423 folder 1.

19 Irwin Miller, letter to Harry Weese, October 13, 1987, box 472, folder 6.

20 Paul Rand, *A Look at Architecture* (Columbus, IN: Columbus Area Chamber of Commerce, 2000); design of twenty-one schools during

this half-century was quite broadly spread across a variety of architects, as per Cummins Engine Foundation's agreement with the Columbus School Board; no single architect did more than two schools.

21 *Columbus (IN) Republic*, March 2, 1998, box 266, folder 5.

22 Rand, 1999.

23 Lee Hamilton, interview with the author, August 9, 2012.

24 Irwin Miller, letter to president of the Fort Wayne Bank, June 19, 1974, box 283, folder 4; emphasis is author's.

25 Box 22, folder 1, March 27, 1966.

26 *Columbus (IN) Republic*, January 22, 1982.

27 Irwin Miller, letter to Robert Osborn, March 18, 1976, box 468, folder 8.

28 Irwin Miller, letter to William Scranton, December 15, 1972, box 391, folder 2.

29 Box 124, folder 1, April 21, 1971.

30 Box 184, folder 8, April 20, 1971.

31 Box 184, folder 7.

Chapter 8

1 Ed Booth, interview with the author, February 8, 2012.

2 William Miller, interview, October 5, 2012.

3 Box 24, folder 5.

4 William Miller, interview, October 5, 2012.

5 James A. Henderson (interview with author, October 9, 2012), though he enjoyed visiting with Cummins's distributors.

6 Walt Divan, interview with the author, May 21, 2012.

7 Miller made one trip, spring of 1975; Cruikshank, 373; by contrast his VP of finance, John A. Hackett, went there fourteen times between 1974 and 1988, letter from Hackett to the author, March 21, 2007.

8 Fred Reams, interview with the author, September 6, 2012.

9 B. Joseph White, interview with the author, April 10, 2012.

10 William Miller, interview, October 5, 2012.

11 Roger Beeden, *Indianapolis News*, Business Section, March 21, 1949.

12 Hoffman, 7.

13 Box 175, folders 3–11.

[14] Box 177, folder 7.

[15] Box 497, folders 7–8.

[16] Disagreement over role of women and rite of Baptism, mainly.

[17] Watkins, 300.

[18] Box 47, folder 1.

[19] Doug Eckhart, interview with the author, December 18, 2012.

[20] J. I. Miller, interview with Geoffrey Kabaservice, December 18, 1991, box 448, folder 11.

[21] Henry "Sam" Chauncey Jr., interviews with the author, July 31, 2012 and November 1, 2012.

[22] Box 466, folder 9.

[23] Geoffrey Kabaservice, *The Guardians* (New York: Henry Holt, 2004), 217.

[24] Reverend Lanny Lawler, interview with the author, June 13, 2013.

[25] Box 519, folder 1.

[26] Box 47, folder 5.

[27] Box 3, folder 5.

[28] Box 487, folder 1.

[29] Box 490, folder 2.

[30] Box 519, folder 1.

[31] Box 336, folder 4.

[32] Irwin Miller, letter, March 21, 1961, box 319, folder 7.

[33] Watkins, 133.

[34] Box 523, folder 7.

[35] Box 331, folder 1.

[36] Floyd Legler, letter to Irwin Miller, February 16, 1983, box 281, folder 5.

[37] Box 319, folder 9.

Chapter 9

[1] Box 237, folder 5, February 13, 1974.

[2] Steve Roberts, *Esquire* (October 1967); "Is it too late for a man of Honesty, High Purpose, and Intelligence to be elected President of the United States in 1967."

[3] The Block, Cummins Inc. social media news hub.

[4] Roberts, *Esquire*.

5   *The Christian Century* (October 25, 1961): 1285–1286.

6   William Miller, interview, October 5, 2012.

7   Box 320, folder 8.

8   Ibid, 220.

9   Ibid, 167.

10   Ibid, 328.

11   Ibid, 174.

12   Henry "Sam" Chauncey Jr., interview with the author, July 31, 2012.

13   Kabaservice, *The Guardians*, 220.

14   Box 443, folder 10.

15   A fellow, not a trustee.

16   Kabaservice, *The Guardians*, 259–260.

17   Ibid, 328.

18   Ibid, 368.

19   YDB Convocation, box 456, folder 8:

20   Geoffrey Kabaservice, *The Guardians*, 274.

21   Ibid, 275.

22   Ford Foundation, internal interview, February 13, 1974, box 237, folder 5.

23   Ford Foundation, oral history project, October 2, 1972, box 272, folder 5.

24   J. I. Miller, interview with Geoffrey Kabaservice, February 17, 2001.

25   Kabaservice, *The Guardians*, 271.

26   Ibid, 69.

27   Ibid, 277.

28   Box 422, folder 4, February 22, 1984.

29   Donald S. Perkins, interview with the author, September 17, 2012.

30   J. I. Miller, interview with Robert Lynn, February–March 1991, box 278, folder 2.

31   Sarla Kalsi, telephone conversation with the author, March 15, 2014.

32   Fred Reams, interview with the author, March 11, 2014.

33   Reams, interviews with the author, September 16, 2012, and March 11, 2014. Reams's accomplishments with Cummins's pension fund get no mention in Cruikshank, funnily enough.

34   Garnett Keith, interview with the author, March 13, 2014.

35   Garnett Keith, interview with the author, March 23, 2014..

Chapter 10

1. Box 374, folder 4.
2. Ibid.
3. Box 523, folder 1.
4. Cruikshank, 201.
5. Cruikshank, 36.
6. Cruikshank, 202.
7. Cruikshank, 203.
8. Cruikshank, 107; an alert, independent board of directors with a broad range of background, including engine design, surely could have helped.
9. Cruikshank, 223.
10. Cruikshank, 195.
11. Not the turnover it seems, since one would be transferred to head operations and another died.
12. Cruikshank, 208.
13. *Businessweek* (October 5, 1963): 94.
14. Ibid.
15. Ibid.
16. Cruikshank, 208.
17. William Miller, e-mail to the author, June 5, 2013.
18. Laurence R. Hoagland, interview with the author, October 24, 2012; Hoagland later was VP of finance at Cummins and ultimately oversaw the endowment at Hewlett Foundation.
19. William Miller, e-mail to the author, June 5, 2013.
20. Cruikshank, footnote 81, chapter 6.
21. "The Cough in Cummins Engine," *Fortune* (August 1968).
22. Cruikshank, 311.
23. Cruikshank, 214.
24. Miller would write years later to McGeorge Bundy, president of the Ford Foundation, that "[his] service on the membership committee *per se* put him in touch with dozens of 'leaders' across the world as they looked for board members-the 12-year term cause of regular turn-over"; box 237, folder 4.

25 Cummins Engine annual reports, box 3, folders 3 and 6. (As we'll see, in the 1970s, Cummins would add to its board six more outsiders, including a black and a woman.)

26 Cruikshank,152.

27 Cruikshank, 156.

28 Sixty years of Cummins financial data are appended at the rear of this book, prepared by Hari Chelluri, longtime assistant to the author

29 Watkins, 171

30 Sam Chauncey, interview by the author, July 31, 2012.

Chapter 11

1 Box 509, folder 2, December 27, 1963.

2 Box 507, folder 3, January 6, 1964.

3 Roberts, *Esquire.*

4 Roberts, *Esquire,* 173.

5 Hamilton, interview.

6 Roberts, *Esquire,* 173.

7 Box 509, folder 5, January 5, 1965.

8 Introduction, ISM catalogue.

9 Robert Stewart, taped interview, November 13, 1995.

10 Stewart, taped interview.

11 Box 465, folder 9, July 15, 1944.

12 Box 465, folder 10, November 4, 1944.

13 Box 465, folder 9, November 4, 1944.

14 Box 508, folder 5, March 1, 1954.

15 Box 509, folder 9, October 24, 1960.

16 Box 509, folder 4, October 2, 1964.

17 Box 509, folder 5, January 5, 65.

18 Miller had just promoted Tull to president in February 1960 after terminating Robert J. Huthsteiner. "Miller loathed firing people, but… Cummins had outgrown Huthsteiner." Cruikshank, 195.

19 Eckhart, interview; Eckhart explained they would fly out of Walesboro, Indiana (or, if really bad weather, Seymour, Indiana, which had a control

tower), until 1972 when the city of Columbus obtained Bakalar Field from the US government.

20   Box 261, folder 1; box 262, folder 6.
21   Box 222, folder 1, Maybe 15, 1965.
22   Box 222, folder 1, June 8, 1965.
23   Box 261, folder 1.
24   *New York Post*, October 5, 1971, box 502, folder 7.
25   Henderson, interview, February 23, 2012.
26   Kabaservice, *The Guardians*, 435.
27   *New York Post*, June 27, 1973, box 502, folder 7.
28   Cruikshank, 322–323.
29   Box 472, folder 5, September 26, 1980.
30   Box 126, folder 6, September 13, 1993.
31   Box 391, folder 1, July 1971.
32   Box 534, folder 6, September 1971.
33   Box 535, folder 11, May 1973.
34   Box 545, folder 18, April 1993.

Chapter 12

1   Cruikshank, 240.
2   James Henderson, letter to Irwin Miller, June 13, 1968, box 80, folder 3; the name of Henry B. Schacht, who would ultimately be Miller's top choice, is not mentioned until the last paragraph of this three-page letter, almost an aside—"One alternative would be to move H. B. Schacht [then VP of international and subsidiaries] to Vaughn's job."
3   Box 80, folder 3, November 16, 1968.
4   Box 80, folder 3, spring 1969 (probably April).
5   Irwin Miller, letter to Donald R. Smith, October 11, 1972, box 472, folder 8.
6   Keith, interview, March 23, 2012.
7   Richard P. Vancil, letter, "Passing the Baton at Cummins Engine," box 37, folder 7.
8   Box 80, folder 3.
9   James A. Henderson, Interview with the author, June 8, 2012.
10   Jim Collins, *Good to Great* (New York: Harper Business, 2001).

11 Henderson, interview with the author, June 8, 2012.

12 Richard F. Vancil, letter to Mr. Miller, et. al. July 22, 1986; Irwin Miller, letter to Richard F. Vancil, July 30, 1986; box 37, folder 7.

13 Cummins annual reports

14 Donald B. Perkins, interview with the author, September 12, 2012.

15 This collection would fetch $118 million at auction in London, June 2008 (www.Christies.com/lotfinder).

16 Box 1003, folder 11.

17 Box 545, folder 5 (Miller would be 82 the next month).

18 Cruikshank, 262.

19 Cruikshank, 277.

20 Cruikshank. 264.

21 Cruikshank, 263.

22 Tom Conway, interview with the author, March 14, 2014.

23 Cruikshank, 285.

24 Essentially, R&D facility for B and C engines.

25 Box 65, folder 3.

26 Kirloskar was Cummins's joint venture partner in India.

27 Box 472, folder 9.

Chapter 13

1   Cruikshank, 12.

2   Donald S. Perkins, interview with the author, September 18, 2012.

3   Fred Reams, interview with the author, September 17, 2012.

4   Hanafee, interview.

5   James A. Henderson, interview with the author, May 22, 2012.

6   James A. Henderson, interview with the author, February 4, 2013.

7   Cruikshank, 298–303.

8   Irwin Miller, speech #104, "U.S. Government Policy toward South Africa," September 11, 1986, box 5, folder 2.

9   Cruikshank, Page 6.

10 John T. Hackett, letter to the author, March 21, 2007, Indiana Historical Society, CEMR Collection.

11 1991 Cummins Annual Report.

[12] Perkins, interview, September 18, 2012.

[13] It may have been because, in a 2007 research report, including a short history of Cummins, the author referred to the Schacht-Henderson hegemony as "Miller Lite"!

[14] A very, very real threat, as offering huge price mark-downs and similar quality, Japanese machine tool-makers (backed by their government) savaged their US counterparts in the 1980s. As reference, Max Holland, *When the Machine Stalled* (Boston: Harvard Business School, 1989).

[15] Box 545, folder 5.

[16] John T. Hackett, letter to CEMR, March 21, 2007, CEMR collection.

[17] Cruikshank, 259.

[18] Cruikshank, 488.

[19] William Miller, interview with the author, March 15, 2014.

[20] Box 545, folder 26.

Chapter 14

[1] William Miller, interview with the author, March 8, 2014.

[2] J. I. Miller, interview with Geoffrey Kabaservice, December 14, 1991, box 448, folder 11.

[3] Readers, especially Midwesterners, will recall that Giamatti would leave Yale, in turn, to become commissioner of baseball, famously banishing Pete Rose from the sport for gambling.

[4] Box 470, folder 9.

[5] Box 436, folder 3.

[6] Box 436, folder 1.

[7] Box 478, folder 5.

[8] Box 449, folder 4.

[9] Ibid.; Robert S. Tangeman, Clementine's late husband, who had died in 1964, taught for years at UTS.

[10] Irwin Miller, letter to A. Bartlett Giamatti, December 1, 1981, box 449, folder 7.

[11] Clementine Tangeman, letter to Kingman Brewster, May 10, 1973, box 473, folder 3.

[12] Irwin Miller, letter to Dr. Jon D. Bailey, May 8, 1979, box 449, folder 4.

13   Irwin Miller, letter to A. Bartlett Giamatti, December 1, 1981, box 473, folder 3.

14   Irwin Miller, letter to William K. Zinsser, May 24, 1977, box 447, folder 1.

15   Irwin Miller, letter to Sam Chauncey, May 3, 1979, box 471, folder 5.

16   Sam Chauncey, interview with the author, July 31, 2012.

17   Watkins 171.

18   Box 169, folder 3.

19   Ibid.

20   Watkins, 194–195.

21   Watkins, 195.

22   Box 171, folder 1, October 3, 1986.

23   Irwin Miller, letter to Dr. Harold E. Fey, October 14, 1987, box 230, folder 6.

24   Irwin Miller, letter to T. J. Liggett, September 28, 1984, box 594, folder 4; Clementine Tangeman wrote in 1992, "My total giving to CTS… has been about $16 million," box 171, folder 6.

25   Box 172, folder 5, December 5, 1985.

26   Irwin Miller, letter to Dr. Harold E. Fey, October 14, 1987, box 230, folder 6.

27   Box 594, folder 4.

28   Marilyn Keiser, interview with the author, December 10, 2012.

29   Watkins, 239.

Chapter 15

1   Cruikshank, 414.

2   Cruikshank, 417.

3   *Columbus (IN) Republic*, July 18, 1989.

4   Donald S. Perkins, interview with the author, September 17, 2012.

5   Cruikshank, 424–425.

6   Irwin Miller, letter to Henry Schacht, February 25, 1997.

7   Box 10, folder 8: "Prepared for use of counsel at Simpson Thacher."

8   Box 479, folder 5, June 11, 1993.

9   Box 519, folder 1.

[10] Irwin Miller, remarks, Pritzker Exhibit preview, Indianapolis Museum of Art, May 20, 1994, box 545, folder 21.

[11] 1990 Cummins annual report.

[12] 1989 Cummins annual report.

[13] Cruikshank, 436; parenthetically, on April 18, 1996, Komatsu *did* purchase 446,464 shares of Cummins Stock for $20.3 million from the estate of Clementine M. Tangeman, who had died that January, box 480, folder 9.

[14] Box 66, folder 2.

[15] John Dorenbusch, interview with the author, May 3, 2014; John Dorenbusch was a longtime executive with Miller family businesses.

[16] Cummins annual reports.

[17] Irwin Miller, handwritten note responding to angry letter from anonymous employee, box 18, folder 6.

[18] Irwin Miller, speech #135, board of directors dinner, July 13,1992, box 519, folder 1.

[19] Box 69, folder 1.

[20] Box 481, folder 4.

[21] Hanafee, *Red, Black and Global*, 33.

[22] Hanafee, *Red, Black and Global*, 39.

Chapter 16

[1] Box 545, folder 34.

[2] Box 29, folder 6.

[3] Box 450, folder 1.

[4] Box 390, folder 1.

[5] Caroline McKin Spicer, interview with the author.

[6] Irwin Miller, letter to Mrs. Maynard Mack, October 1, 2000, box 483, folder 3.

[7] Box 484, folder 4.

[8] Caroline McKin Spicer, interview with the author.

[9] Benjamin Wever, interview with the author, January 12, 2013.

[10] Ibid.

[11] Box 482, folder 4.

[12] Hanafee, *Red, Black, and Global*, 81.

Cummins Engine Co. / Cummins Inc. Financial Data

Appendix

Prepared by Hari Chelluri, Financial Accountant

Summary financial data for Cummins Engine Co. / Cummins Inc. for the years 1951 – 2011. Historical data obtained from company annual report filings and authors estimates where company data was not available.

Cummins Engine Co. / Cummins Inc. Financial Data

Abridged Income Statement	1951	1952	1953	1954	1955	1956	1957	1958	1959	1960
Sales ($MM)	61	55	56	59	81	106	111	109	147	136
Sales - yr/yr		(9.8%)	2.5%	5.7%	36.9%	30.6%	5.1%	(2.2%)	35.2%	(7.6%)
Gross Profit	16	11	13	15	24	30	31	29	46	40
Gross Margin	26.4%	20.1%	22.4%	25.9%	29.4%	28.2%	28.1%	26.8%	31.6%	29.2%
SG&A (inc R&D until '58)	(7)	(7)	(9)	(9)	(14)	(18)	(20)	(16)	(23)	(20)
as % of sales	11%	13%	16%	16%	18%	17%	18%	15%	15%	15%
Research & Development								(4)	(6)	(6)
as % of sales								3%	4%	4%
Operating Income	9	4	4	6	10	12	11	9	18	14
Operating Margin	15.6%	6.8%	6.7%	10.3%	11.7%	11.3%	9.9%	8.4%	12.4%	10.1%
Interest Expense	(0)	(0)	(0)	(0)	(0)	(0)	(1)	(1)	(1)	(1)
Reported Net Income	3	2	2	3	5	6	5	4	8	6

Analytics	1951	1952	1953	1954	1955	1956	1957	1958	1959	1960
Net Margin	4.5%	3.4%	2.9%	4.9%	5.6%	5.4%	4.6%	3.6%	5.6%	4.4%
Earnings Per Share*	$0.06	$0.04	$0.03	$0.06	$0.10	$0.12	$0.11	$0.08	$0.17	$0.13
Dividends Per Share	$0.01	$0.01	$0.01	$0.01	$0.01	$0.02	$0.02	$0.03	$0.03	$0.03
Stock Dividends & Splits	10%			5%	5 for 4	5 for 4	10%	5%		2 for 1: 5%

Earnings per share data excludes extraordinary items

Leverage / Liquidity	1951	1952	1953	1954	1955	1956	1957	1958	1959	1960
Debt / Total Equity	26%	42%	39%	36%	34%	34%	54%	66%	53%	46%
Current Ratio	2.1x	3.6x	3.8x	4.0x	3.0x	2.5x	2.5x	3.4x	2.6x	2.5x
Interest Coverage	185.1x	24.6x	15.2x	27.1x	35.0x	46.3x	16.4x	8.8x	16.0x	11.9x

Returns	1951	1952	1953	1954	1955	1956	1957	1958	1959	1960
Return on Common Equity	18.7%	11.6%	9.3%	16.1%	20.9%	21.6%	16.8%	11.7%	20.4%	13.4%
Pretax Operating Return on Assets	32.6%	13.0%	12.5%	19.2%	25.9%	24.8%	17.5%	13.3%	23.0%	16.1%

Capitalization	1951	1952	1953	1954	1955	1956	1957	1958	1959	1960
Debt	20.6%	29.5%	28.2%	26.7%	25.2%	25.4%	35.2%	39.7%	34.8%	31.7%
Preferred	6.0%	4.4%	4.1%	3.4%	0.0%	0.0%	0.0%	0.0%	0.0%	0.0%
Equity & Minority Interest	73.4%	66.0%	67.7%	69.9%	74.8%	74.6%	64.8%	60.3%	65.2%	68.3%
Total	100.0%	100.0%	100.0%	100.0%	100.0%	100.0%	100.0%	100.0%	100.0%	100.0%

	1951	1952	1953	1954	1955	1956	1957	1958	1959	1960
# of Employees	3,000	2,945	2,961	2,900	3,248	4,128	3,938	4,004	6,304	5,018
Year/Year Chg in Employment		(2%)	1%	(2%)	12%	27%	(5%)	2%	57%	(20%)

1

Cummins Engine Co. / Cummins Inc. Financial Data

Abridged Income Statement	1961	1962	1963	1964	1965	1966	1967	1968	1969	1970
Sales ($MM)	129	167	194	222	281	331	306	368	412	449
Sales - yr/yr	*(4.8%)*	*29.4%*	*16.1%*	*14.1%*	*26.6%*	*17.9%*	*(7.5%)*	*20.0%*	*12.2%*	*8.8%*
Gross Profit	40	56	68	75	88	101	80	109	128	140
Gross Margin	*30.8%*	*33.2%*	*34.7%*	*33.8%*	*31.3%*	*30.6%*	*26.0%*	*29.7%*	*31.0%*	*31.2%*
SG&A (inc R&D until '58)	(19)	(26)	(32)	(34)	(43)	(53)	(55)	(63)	(75)	(82)
as % of sales	*15%*	*16%*	*17%*	*15%*	*15%*	*16%*	*18%*	*17%*	*18%*	*18%*
Research & Development	(6)	(7)	(7)	(13)	(16)	(18)	(17)	(15)	(15)	(19)
as % of sales	*4%*	*4%*	*4%*	*6%*	*6%*	*5%*	*6%*	*4%*	*4%*	*4%*
Operating Income	15	23	28	28	29	30	8	31	37	40
Operating Margin	*12.0%*	*13.7%*	*14.4%*	*12.8%*	*10.5%*	*9.0%*	*2.5%*	*8.4%*	*9.0%*	*8.8%*
Interest Expense	(1)	(2)	(1)	(1)	(2)	(3)	(4)	(5)	(4)	(4)
Reported Net Income	6	11	14	14	15	16	4	13	18	20
Net Margin	*4.9%*	*6.3%*	*7.0%*	*6.4%*	*5.4%*	*4.9%*	*1.2%*	*3.6%*	*4.4%*	*4.6%*
*Earnings Per Share**	*$0.13*	*$0.22*	*$0.28*	*$0.30*	*$0.31*	*$0.33*	*$0.07*	*$0.26*	*$0.34*	*$0.38*
Dividends Per Share	*$0.03*	*$0.04*	*$0.05*	*$0.06*	*$0.06*	*$0.08*	*$0.08*	*$0.08*	*$0.09*	*$0.10*
Stock Dividends & Splits	*10%*	*5 for 4*		*4 for 3*				*10%*	*10%*	

* Earnings per share data exludes extraordinary items

Analytics	1961	1962	1963	1964	1965	1966	1967	1968	1969	1970
Leverage / Liquidity										
Debt / Total Equity	43%	30%	20%	29%	46%	63%	74%	53%	55%	64%
Current Ratio	3.1x	2.8x	2.8x	2.1x	2.3x	2.7x	3.1x	2.6x	2.2x	2.3x
Interest Coverage	14.5x	14.1x	33.2x	29.0x	17.7x	11.7x	1.8x	6.6x	10.0x	9.3x
Returns										
Return on Common Equity	12.6%	18.1%	19.3%	17.4%	16.1%	15.1%	3.4%	11.2%	13.9%	14.0%
Pretax Operating Return on Assets	16.9%	21.9%	23.7%	18.6%	15.5%	12.7%	3.2%	12.2%	13.3%	12.3%
Capitalization										
Debt	29.9%	23.4%	16.4%	22.4%	31.4%	38.8%	42.4%	34.6%	35.6%	39.1%
Preferred	0.0%	0.0%	0.0%	0.0%	0.0%	0.0%	0.0%	0.0%	0.0%	0.0%
Equity & Minority Interest	70.1%	76.6%	83.6%	77.6%	68.6%	61.2%	57.6%	65.4%	64.4%	60.9%
Total	100.0%	100.0%	100.0%	100.0%	100.0%	100.0%	100.0%	100.0%	100.0%	100.0%
# of Employees	5,512	6,900	7,550	9,905	11,135	13,024	11,982	14,068	13,981	14,544
Year/Year Chg in Employment	*10%*	*25%*	*9%*	*31%*	*12%*	*17%*	*(8%)*	*17%*	*(1%)*	*4%*

2

Cummins Engine Co. / Cummins Inc. Financial Data

Abridged Income Statement	1971	1972	1973	1974	1975	1976	1977	1978	1979	1980
Sales ($MM)	492	521	686	833	762	1,031	1,264	1,521	1,771	1,667
Sales - yr/yr	9.7%	5.9%	31.6%	21.5%	(8.6%)	35.3%	22.6%	20.3%	16.4%	(5.9%)
Gross Profit	151	145	205	234	197	332	410	469	515	428
Gross Margin	30.7%	27.7%	29.9%	28.1%	25.9%	32.2%	32.5%	30.9%	29.1%	25.7%
SG&A (inc R&D until '58)	(92)	(104)	(131)	(137)	(131)	(171)	(233)	(296)	(349)	(332)
as % of sales	19%	20%	19%	16%	17%	17%	18%	19%	20%	20%
Research & Development	(22)	(23)	(26)	(29)	(29)	(33)	(41)	(42)	(59)	(62)
as % of sales	4%	4%	4%	3%	4%	3%	3%	3%	3%	4%
Operating Income	38	17	47	68	37	128	136	130	107	34
Operating Margin	7.7%	3.3%	6.9%	8.1%	4.8%	12.4%	10.8%	8.6%	6.0%	2.0%
Interest Expense	(5)	(7)	(12)	(19)	(20)	(13)	(12)	(14)	(23)	(29)
Reported Net Income	21	8	26	24	0	59	67	64	58	(11)
Net Margin	4.4%	1.6%	3.8%	2.9%	0.1%	5.7%	5.3%	4.2%	3.3%	(0.7%)
Earnings Per Share*	$0.39	$0.15	$0.44	$0.40	$0.11	$0.93	$1.00	$0.93	$0.84	($0.16)
Dividends Per Share	$0.11	$0.12	$0.12	$0.12	$0.13	$0.13	$0.18	$0.21	$0.23	$0.23
Stock Dividends & Splits										

Earnings per share data exludes extraordinary items

Analytics	1971	1972	1973	1974	1975	1976	1977	1978	1979	1980
Leverage / Liquidity										
Debt / Total Equity	51%	75%	99%	110%	96%	54%	39%	50%	50%	58%
Current Ratio	2.6x	1.9x	2.0x	1.8x	2.2x	1.7x	2.0x	1.7x	1.8x	1.9x
Interest Coverage	7.0x	2.4x	4.0x	3.5x	1.8x	9.5x	11.6x	9.1x	4.7x	1.2x
Returns										
Return on Common Equity	12.2%	4.5%	13.2%	11.1%	0.2%	21.8%	17.4%	14.9%	12.2%	(2.4%)
Pretax Operating Return on Assets	10.7%	4.0%	8.7%	9.8%	5.9%	17.7%	16.7%	13.4%	9.7%	3.0%
Capitalization										
Debt	33.7%	42.9%	49.6%	52.3%	49.0%	35.2%	28.0%	33.5%	33.1%	36.6%
Preferred	0.0%	0.0%	0.0%	4.9%	5.5%	5.7%	0.0%	0.0%	0.0%	0.0%
Equity & Minority Interest	66.3%	57.1%	50.4%	42.7%	45.5%	59.2%	72.0%	66.5%	66.9%	63.4%
Total	100.0%	100.0%	100.0%	100.0%	100.0%	100.0%	100.0%	100.0%	100.0%	100.0%
# of Employees	15,014	16,509	19,516	20,364	17,971	20,932	22,119	23,298	23,849	21,214
Year/Year Chg in Employment	3%	10%	18%	4%	(12%)	16%	6%	5%	2%	(11%)

3

Cummins Engine Co. / Cummins Inc. Financial Data

Abridged Income Statement	1981	1982	1983	1984	1985	1986	1987	1988	1989	1990
Sales ($MM)	1,962	1,587	1,605	2,326	2,146	2,304	2,767	3,310	3,511	3,462
Sales - yr/yr	17.7%	(19.1%)	1.1%	44.9%	(7.7%)	7.3%	20.1%	19.6%	6.1%	(1.4%)
Gross Profit	558	429	482	777	609	590	696	756	789	605
Gross Margin	28.4%	27.0%	30.0%	33.4%	28.4%	25.6%	25.2%	22.8%	22.5%	17.5%
SG&A (inc R&D until '58)	(351)	(336)	(316)	(378)	(381)	(431)	(468)	(540)	(559)	(488)
as % of sales	16%	21%	20%	16%	18%	19%	17%	16%	16%	14%
Research & Development	(89)	(94)	(100)	(106)	(117)	(155)	(149)	(156)	(175)	(144)
as % of sales	5%	6%	6%	5%	5%	7%	5%	5%	5%	4%
Operating Income	119	(1)	66	293	111	5	79	60	55	(27)
Operating Margin	6.0%	(0.1%)	4.1%	12.6%	5.2%	0.2%	2.9%	1.8%	1.6%	(0.8%)
Interest Expense	(32)	(35)	(34)	(32)	(28)	(45)	(52)	(52)	(52)	(44)
Reported Net Income	115	8	5	188	50	(107)	14	(63)	(6)	(136)
Net Margin	5.9%	0.5%	0.3%	8.1%	2.3%	(4.7%)	0.5%	(1.9%)	(0.2%)	(4.0%)
Earnings Per Share*	$1.40	$0.03	$0.05	$2.42	$0.65	($1.31)	$0.07	($0.84)	($0.19)	($1.81)
Dividends Per Share	$0.23	$0.25	$0.25	$0.26	$0.28	$0.28	$0.28	$0.28	$0.28	$0.28
Stock Dividends & Splits										

Earnings per share data exludes extraordinary items

Analytics	1981	1982	1983	1984	1985	1986	1987	1988	1989	1990
Leverage / Liquidity										
Debt / Total Equity	66%	65%	59%	41%	41%	58%	50%	72%	123%	69%
Current Ratio	1.9x	1.7x	1.7x	1.8x	1.6x	1.4x	1.4x	1.4x	1.3x	1.4x
Interest Coverage	3.7x	0.0x	1.9x	9.3x	3.9x	0.1x	1.5x	1.2x	1.1x	-0.6x
Returns										
Return on Common Equity	22.9%	1.7%	1.0%	29.0%	7.1%	(18.2%)	0.9%	(13.5%)	(12.7%)	(40.4%)
Pretax Operating Return on Assets	8.4%	-0.1%	5.3%	19.5%	6.5%	0.2%	3.9%	2.9%	2.7%	-1.3%
Capitalization										
Debt	39.6%	39.3%	37.2%	29.2%	29.3%	36.6%	33.4%	42.0%	55.1%	41.0%
Preferred	4.8%	5.4%	0.5%	0.1%	0.0%	9.5%	9.5%	9.5%	24.2%	12.2%
Equity & Minority Interest	55.5%	55.3%	62.3%	70.7%	70.7%	53.9%	57.1%	48.5%	20.7%	46.8%
Total	100.0%	100.0%	100.0%	100.0%	100.0%	100.0%	100.0%	100.0%	100.0%	100.0%
# of Employees	22,788	18,932	18,615	21,028	19,600	23,400	24,500	26,100	25,100	24,900
Year/Year Chg in Employment	7%	(17%)	(2%)	13%	(7%)	19%	5%	7%	(4%)	(1%)

4

Cummins Engine Co. / Cummins Inc. Financial Data

Abridged Income Statement	1991	1992	1993	1994	1995	1996	1997	1998	1999	2000
Sales ($MM)	3,406	3,749	4,248	4,737	5,245	5,257	5,625	6,266	6,639	6,597
Sales - yr/yr	(1.6%)	10.1%	13.3%	11.5%	10.7%	0.2%	7.0%	11.4%	6.0%	(0.6%)
Gross Profit	629	843	1,037	1,187	1,271	1,185	1,280	1,249	1,418	1,259
Gross Margin	*18.5%*	*22.5%*	*24.4%*	*25.0%*	*24.2%*	*22.5%*	*22.8%*	*19.9%*	*21.4%*	*19.1%*
SG&A (inc R&D until '58)	(472)	(533)	(579)	(641)	(692)	(725)	(744)	(787)	(781)	(776)
as % of sales	*14%*	*14%*	*14%*	*14%*	*13%*	*14%*	*13%*	*13%*	*12%*	*12%*
Research & Development	(147)	(180)	(210)	(238)	(263)	(252)	(260)	(255)	(245)	(244)
as % of sales	*4%*	*5%*	*5%*	*5%*	*5%*	*5%*	*5%*	*4%*	*4%*	*4%*
Operating Income	9	131	248	308	316	208	276	207	392	239
Operating Margin	*0.3%*	*3.5%*	*5.8%*	*6.5%*	*6.0%*	*4.0%*	*4.9%*	*3.3%*	*5.9%*	*3.6%*
Interest Expense	(43)	(41)	(36)	(18)	(13)	(18)	(26)	(71)	(75)	(96)
Reported Net Income	(14)	(190)	177	253	224	160	212	(21)	160	8
Net Margin	*(0.4%)*	*(5.1%)*	*4.2%*	*5.3%*	*4.3%*	*3.0%*	*3.8%*	*(0.3%)*	*2.4%*	*0.1%*
Earnings Per Share*	($0.62)	$0.44	$1.19	$1.53	$1.38	$1.00	$1.37	($0.14)	$1.03	$0.05
Dividends Per Share	$0.09	$0.03	$0.05	$0.16	$0.25	$0.25	$0.27	$0.28	$0.28	$0.30
Stock Dividends & Splits			2 for 1							

* Earnings per share data excludes extraordinary items

Analytics

Leverage / Liquidity	1991	1992	1993	1994	1995	1996	1997	1998	1999	2000
Debt / Total Equity	66%	83%	29%	22%	19%	32%	46%	96%	85%	90%
Current Ratio	1.3x	1.4x	1.5x	1.5x	1.3x	1.5x	1.6x	1.8x	1.7x	1.5x
Interest Coverage	0.2x	3.2x	6.8x	17.6x	24.3x	11.6x	10.6x	2.9x	5.2x	2.8x

Returns	1991	1992	1993	1994	1995	1996	1997	1998	1999	2000
Return on Common Equity	(5.0%)	(62.6%)	23.9%	23.6%	18.9%	12.3%	15.5%	(1.7%)	11.8%	0.6%
Pretax Operating Return on Assets	0.5%	5.9%	10.4%	11.4%	10.3%	6.2%	7.3%	4.6%	8.3%	5.3%

Capitalization	1991	1992	1993	1994	1995	1996	1997	1998	1999	2000
Debt	39.7%	45.4%	22.3%	17.8%	15.6%	24.0%	31.5%	49.1%	46.0%	47.2%
Preferred	11.1%	12.5%	10.6%	0.0%	0.0%	0.0%	0.0%	0.0%	0.0%	0.0%
Equity & Minority Interest	49.2%	42.1%	67.1%	82.2%	84.4%	76.0%	68.5%	50.9%	54.0%	52.8%
Total	100.0%	100.0%	100.0%	100.0%	100.0%	100.0%	100.0%	100.0%	100.0%	100.0%

	1991	1992	1993	1994	1995	1996	1997	1998	1999	2000
# of Employees	22,900	23,400	23,600	25,600	24,300	23,500	26,300	28,300	28,500	28,000
Year/Year Chg in Employment	(8%)	2%	1%	8%	(5%)	(3%)	12%	8%	1%	(2%)

5

Cummins Engine Co. / Cummins Inc. Financial Data

Abridged Income Statement	2000	2001	2002	2003	2004	2005	2006	2007	2008	2009	2010	2011
Sales ($MM)	6,597	5,681	5,853	6,296	8,438	9,918	11,362	13,048	14,342	10,800	13,226	18,048
Sales - yr/yr	(0.6%)	(13.9%)	3.0%	7.6%	34.0%	17.5%	14.6%	14.8%	9.9%	(24.7%)	22.5%	36.5%
Gross Profit	1,259	1,021	1,045	1,123	1,680	2,186	2,595	2,556	2,940	2,189	3,168	4,589
Gross Margin	19.1%	18.0%	17.9%	17.8%	19.9%	22.0%	22.8%	19.6%	20.5%	20.1%	24.0%	25.4%
SG&A (inc R&D until '58)	(778)	(728)	(736)	(830)	(1,015)	(1,145)	(1,283)	(1,296)	(1,450)	(1,239)	(1,487)	(1,837)
as % of sales	12%	13%	13%	13%	12%	12%	11%	10%	10%	11%	11%	10%
Research & Development	(244)	(220)	(201)	(200)	(241)	(278)	(321)	(329)	(422)	(362)	(414)	(629)
as % of sales	4%	4%	3%	3%	3%	3%	3%	3%	3%	3%	3%	3%
Operating Income	239	73	108	93	424	763	991	931	1,068	568	1,267	2,123
Operating Margin	3.6%	1.3%	1.8%	1.5%	5.0%	7.7%	8.7%	7.1%	7.4%	5.3%	9.6%	11.8%
Interest Expense	(86)	(76)	(61)	(90)	(113)	(109)	(96)	(58)	(42)	(35)	(40)	(44)
Reported Net Income	8	(91)	103	61	350	550	715	739	755	428	1,040	1,848
Net Margin	0.1%	(1.6%)	1.8%	1.0%	4.1%	5.5%	6.3%	5.7%	5.3%	4.0%	7.9%	10.2%
Earnings Per Share*	$0.05	($0.67)	$0.52	$0.34	$1.85	$2.75	$3.55	$3.70	$3.84	$2.16	$5.28	$9.55
Dividends Per Share	$0.30	$0.30	$0.30	$0.30	$0.30	$0.30	$0.30	$0.43	$0.60	$0.70	$0.88	$1.33
Stock Dividends & Splits								2 for 1; 2 for 1				

*Earnings per share data excludes extraordinary items

Analytics	2000	2001	2002	2003	2004	2005	2006	2007	2008	2009	2010	2011
Leverage / Liquidity												
Debt / Total Equity	90%	92%	135%	151%	117%	73%	29%	20%	22%	17%	16%	12%
Current Ratio	1.5x	1.7x	1.5x	1.5x	1.5x	1.8x	1.9x	1.8x	1.8x	2.1x	1.9x	1.9x
Interest Coverage	2.8x	1.0x	1.8x	1.0x	3.8x	7.0x	10.3x	16.1x	25.4x	16.2x	31.7x	48.3x
Returns												
Return on Common Equity	0.6%	(15.7%)	17.9%	6.1%	29.3%	33.6%	28.1%	23.7%	25.3%	11.3%	22.3%	33.6%
Pretax Operating Return on Assets	5.3%	1.7%	2.2%	1.8%	6.5%	11.1%	13.3%	11.4%	12.5%	6.4%	12.2%	18.2%
Capitalization												
Debt	47.2%	48.0%	57.5%	60.1%	54.0%	42.3%	22.4%	16.5%	17.8%	14.4%	13.7%	10.5%
Preferred	0.0%	14.8%	14.7%	0.0%	0.0%	0.0%	0.0%	0.0%	0.0%	0.0%	0.0%	0.0%
Equity & Minority Interest	52.8%	37.3%	27.8%	39.9%	46.0%	57.7%	77.6%	83.5%	82.2%	85.6%	86.3%	89.5%
Total	100.0%	100.0%	100.0%	100.0%	100.0%	100.0%	100.0%	100.0%	100.0%	100.0%	100.0%	100.0%
# of Employees	28,000	24,900	23,700	24,200	28,100	33,500	34,600	37,800	39,800	34,900	39,200	43,900
Year/Year Chg in Employment	(2%)	(11%)	(5%)	2%	16%	19%	3%	9%	5%	(12%)	12%	12%

183

Made in the USA
Monee, IL
15 January 2020